A Soldier's Journey (1940-1945)

A Soldier's Journey (1940-1945)

First Edition
August 2012

Michael John Laekas

ISBN 978-0-9879721-1-8

Library and Archives Canada Cataloguing in Publication

Laekas, Michael John, 1943-
        A soldier's journey (1940-1945) / Michael John Laekas.

Includes bibliographical references.
ISBN 978-0-9865703-7-7 (bound).--ISBN 978-0-9879721-1-8 (pbk.)

        1. Laekas, Jean-Pierre. 2. Canada. Canadian Army. Fusiliers Mont-Royal--Biography.   3. World War, 1939-1945--Canada--Biography.   4. Soldiers--Canada--Biography.   I. Title.

D811.L3225 2012   940.54'8171   C2012-901690-X

Edited and illustrated by Johanne Gervais
Cover design by Johanne Gervais

www.gervais-laekas.com for ordering information

Disclaimer

All people and events in this story are real. Dialogue is written as remembered by the Dieppe raid veterans, except for situations where their memories failed or where they were not present, in which case I have used artistic license to find appropriate words.

French and German narrative has been translated to English for the benefit of the reader.

Preface

This story honours the young French Canadians who, as proud members of Les Fusiliers Mont-Royal, took part in the ill-fated raid on Dieppe, France, on 19 August 1942.

The idea for this book came following a 47-day trip I took in 2011 to follow my father's journey during the Second World War, from his enlistment in 1940 to his repatriation in 1945.

For the 70th anniversary of the Dieppe raid, I felt compelled to document the sacrifices of these young men in this heartfelt and humble commemoration.

Michael John Laekas

Chapter 1
Montréal, Québec
March 1940–May 1940

The effects of the Great Depression lingered. Montréal's industries and businesses struggled and the number of people looking for work far exceeded employment opportunities. A new war in Europe contributed to the uncertain future facing 20-year-old Jean-Pierre Laekas. Jean-Pierre lived with his parents and three sisters in Montréal's east end. After leaving school, he apprenticed at his uncle's garage, but Jean-Pierre believed greater things awaited him. The military's call for volunteers provided him the opportunity to escape a depressed neighbourhood and to embark on a paid adventure.

On 28 March 1940, Jean-Pierre presented himself at the enrolment centre for Les Fusiliers Mont-Royal, a distinguished regiment within the Second Canadian Division and one of the few francophone units in the Canadian Army. An all-volunteer force, the Regiment set high standards for new recruits. They accepted only single men aged 18 to 45 with a minimum height of five feet six inches and no physical disabilities or chronic ailments.

After his initial registration, Jean-Pierre proceeded through a series of lengthy and demanding tests to measure his physical well-being and mental aptitude. At the end of the process, the instructor handed him several sheets of paper then directed him to a room where an enrolment officer sat behind a large table. The officer scanned his test results then took two sheets of a pre-printed form from a neat pile on the corner of the table. Without looking up, he motioned Jean-Pierre towards a wooden chair.

Jean-Pierre sat and nervously waited. The officer meticulously placed a piece of carbon paper between the two sheets, inserted the form in a typewriter, rolled the platen, and carefully aligned the paper using the typewriter's line gauge. Once satisfied with its alignment, he locked the paper in position, looked up at Jean-Pierre, and smiled.

"Right then. Let's get started. Surname first followed by your Christian name in full."

"Laekas," he paused then continued, "Jean-Pierre."

"What's the origin of that name, son?"

"It's Greek."

He nodded his head and continued typing. Once Jean-Pierre answered all the questions, the officer released the form from the typewriter and quickly reviewed his work.

"Please confirm that all the information is correct then sign at the bottom," he said as he slid a fountain pen across the table with the form.

Jean-Pierre started reading the typewritten entries.

"I must warn you that falsifying information is a criminal offense punishable up to six months in prison."

Surprised by the unexpected threat of prison, Jean-Pierre raised his eyes from the paper.

"Don't worry. I can't remember when we last locked up someone for lying," said the officer smiling at the expression on Jean-Pierre's face.

"You spelled Laekas wrong," said Jean-Pierre. "It's L A E KA S not L E A KA S."

After the officer corrected the spelling, Jean-Pierre signed and returned the form.

"Congratulations Fusilier. You're now a member of a very distinguished regiment." He leaned over the desk and shook Jean-Pierre's hand.

"Thank you," Jean-Pierre responded, uncertain of the appropriate response for a Fusilier. *Perhaps I should have saluted.* The thought vanished as the excitement swept over him. *I'm a Fusilier. I'm a member of Les Fusiliers Mont-Royal.* He grinned back at the officer wondering what to do next.

"Here's your transit pass to go home. Report at this address tomorrow morning at 0700 hours."

On his way out, he wondered if 0700 hours meant seven o'clock in the morning. Too excited to wait for a streetcar, he ran down Saint-Denis Street until he reached Ste. Catherine Street. He walked briskly towards the Jacques Cartier Bridge replaying the day's events in his mind. He imagined himself somewhere in Europe on patrol with his regiment searching for the enemy. Bursting with youthful pride, he wanted to shout his enlistment news to everyone he passed. Ten minutes later, he arrived at Beaudry Street. He raced up the metal spiral staircase leading to the triplex's second floor balcony. In a rush, he fumbled with his key to unlock the exterior door. Once inside he quickly closed the door sending its white lace curtain swinging. He ran up the staircase two stairs at a time to the apartment's interior door. It slammed noisily against the doorstop as he swung it open. His startled father rose from his favourite chair, sections of the *Daily Star* falling to the floor.

"Father, I've joined the army!" proclaimed Jean-Pierre.

"My dear boy," he said sitting back down in his chair, "come sit down and tell me what this is all about."

Jean-Pierre recounted in detail his enrolment process and all the tests he went through. His father listened quietly without interrupting. At supper, his sisters were more interested in their personal lives than Jean-Pierre's enlistment. His mother busied herself in the kitchen distraught by her son's news. After supper, Jean-Pierre and his father went for a walk around the neighbourhood. They strolled along Ste. Catherine Street and chatted about everything except the distant war in Europe. While waiting for a truck to pass at an intersection, Michael Laekas tugged on his son's sleeve. Jean-Pierre turned, shocked to see his father's eyes brimming with tears.

"My son, you've always made me proud in everything you've done and I know I can't stop you from leaving. Promise you'll look after yourself."

"I promise, Father."

Michael took his son's face in his hands and kissed him on the cheek. Jean-Pierre put his arm around his father's shoulders and together they walked back to the apartment, alone with their thoughts but glad for the other's company.

The six-storey Motordrome, situated at the corner of Sherbrooke and Saint-Denis Streets, began life as an automobile exposition hall and garage. When the Canadian Army prepared for war, the Fusiliers' Regimental Armoury at 3721 Henri-Julien Avenue could not accommodate the Regiment's projected growth to over 900 men. The army searched for suitable facilities, expropriated the Motordrome, and refurbished it for Les Fusiliers Mont-Royal. The renovated Motordrome included lodging, a kitchen, a dining area, a large drill hall, and administration offices.

At exactly 0700 hours, Jean-Pierre entered the cavernous Motordrome and joined the line of men at the reception desk. The clerk registered his name then issued his military identification tags with the regimental number D61894 inscribed. He followed the long line of inductees to the onsite barber whose clippers sent Jean-Pierre's black locks tumbling over his shoulders. Next, he passed between two lines of nurses for inoculations against cholera, diphtheria, influenza, tetanus, typhoid, typhus, scarlet fever, and smallpox. The man ahead of him fainted when the first needle punctured his skin. Two medical orderlies pulled the prostrate man aside and a nurse gave him the remaining inoculations as he lay on the floor. Following the vaccinations, Jean-Pierre went to the Quartermaster's stores to receive his uniform, underclothes, physical training outfit, boots, helmet, and other accessories. A sergeant led Jean-Pierre and the other recruits, their arms full of army gear, to their bunks in the Motordrome's sleeping quarters.

"Find a bunk, get changed in to your PT gear, and come back to the drill hall in two minutes," he yelled. "Anyone who is late will regret it."

Jean-Pierre threw his newly acquired clothes and equipment on a bunk. He stripped down then got in to his shorts, athletic top, and boots. Dressed, he raced to the drill hall with the other recruits, the stomping of boots on the concrete floor ringing in his ears. He joined a line on one side of the hall where the men proceeded sequentially through a series of stations. Under a drill instructor's steely gaze, each recruit attempted to perform the exercise depicted on a piece of cardboard propped up on a chair. The drill instructors showed no mercy as they shouted and cursed at the recruits. Jean-Pierre knew the sit-ups, push-ups, jumping jacks, and other drills from his school days, but the instructor still managed to find fault with his routines. Despite his excellent physical condition, he struggled to complete the series of exercises. At the end of the day Jean-Pierre, tired but excited, climbed in to his bunk and fell fast asleep.

In the following weeks, Jean-Pierre learned the Regiment's drill sergeant occupied a position just beneath God in the hierarchy of supreme beings. He demanded unquestioning obedience and ran them ragged. Physical conditioning with runs and stationary exercises, hand-to-hand combat, close order drills, manoeuvres, route marches, swimming lessons, and target practice with pistols, rifles, and machine guns occupied their days. Their boots and equipment required continuous polishing. The rigorous program intentionally left the recruits with little leisure time and their drill sergeant's role was clear. Mould the men or break them. Weed out the undesirables, the misfits, the weak, the malingerers, the moaners, and the complainers. Bring the remainder to a state where they followed orders without question, worked together as a cohesive unit, and acted without hesitation or reservation.

The military's structure, order, and discipline appealed to Jean-Pierre and he adapted easily to army life. A few weeks in to basic training, the assignment of recruits to one of the Regiment's six companies took place. Jean-Pierre and 27 other aspiring soldiers led by a sergeant formed #3 platoon in "A" Company. The training continued and the platoon started to bond as a unit.

Maurice Jolicoeur, a tall, broad-shouldered jovial fellow, joined the army's Châteauguay Regiment in June 1939 at the age of 19. Similar to Jean-Pierre, the difficulty in finding work and the military's offer of travel and adventure drew Maurice to join the army. After enlisting, he met a young girl called Pierrette who lived in St. Lambert, almost 25 miles from his regiment. The distance prevented him from seeing her on a regular basis so he transferred to Les Fusiliers Mont-Royal, located only six miles from where Pierrette lived. Assigned to "A" Company, #3 platoon, Maurice quickly developed a unique kinship with Jean-Pierre. They spent most of their leisure time together at the Motordrome and visited each other's families when they took leave.

After two months of basic training, the Regiment received orders to begin advanced training at Camp Valcartier. Officers informed the men in each of the Regiment's six companies then gave the soldiers a 24-hour pass to bid their families good-bye. Jean-Pierre paid a brief visit home letting his family know he would be leaving Montréal then quickly returned to the Regiment.

On 25 May 1940, while waiting to board the troop train at Bonaventure Station, Jean-Pierre and Maurice speculated about the conditions at Valcartier, the duration of their stay at the camp, and the possible destinations of the Regiment thereafter. Once seated, Maurice rested his head against the carriage wall and dozed off. Beside him, Jean-Pierre sat alone with his thoughts and stared out the window at the passing landscape. *I wonder where I'll be in a year's time. Probably on a battlefield somewhere.* The chances of him dying in combat never entered his mind.

Les Fusiliers Mont-Royal Armoury, 3721 Henri-Julien Avenue, Montréal, Québec. *Courtesy of http://lesfusiliersmont-royal.com/*

Private Jean-Pierre Laekas, D61894, Les Fusiliers Mont-Royal. 1940. *Private Collection.*

Chapter 2
Valcartier, Québec
May 1940–June 1940

The relatively benign and comfortable setting of the island of Montréal did little to prepare the Fusiliers for the next phase of their training. Located 170 miles northeast of Montréal on a plateau at the foot of the Laurentian Mountains, the massive Camp Valcartier occupied approximately 130 square miles of rugged terrain. At the camp's base where the men ate, slept, and attended classes, draughty tents provided the troops' only shelter. In the hills, valleys, fields, and rivers where men trained, voracious black flies and unrelenting mosquitoes attacked in swarms. As it had in the First War, the camp served as the training area and departure point for Canadian soldiers destined to serve overseas.

After the three-hour train ride from Montréal, the troops disembarked at the Valcartier station. They quickly formed up by platoons and companies then marched to the immense camp. Endless rows of large canvas bell tents covered the flat plain at the base of the hills. Small one-storey buildings consisting of two wings connected by a common central section stood behind the tents. These "H" Huts served as barracks during the winter season and mess quarters for the officers. The Fusiliers arrived at their tents joining their sister regiments of the Second Canadian Division's Fifth Brigade already at Valcartier, the Black Watch (Royal Highland Regiment) of Canada, Le Regiment de Maisonneuve, and Le Regiment de la Chaudière.

Jean-Pierre shared a large canvas tent with 14 other young recruits. Outside the tented area, he washed in the cold, open communal showers and relieved himself in the long, wooden outhouse containing a trough urinal and 20 back-to-back weathered seats over the foul-smelling collector pit. The thin wool blanket on his bed did little to ward off the damp, cool air that crept into the tent and disturbed his sleep. The drill sergeants started their advanced training with renewed vigour. Whether on the parade ground, in the field, or at the firing range, swarms of black flies and ill-tempered drill instructors followed Jean-Pierre's every move. He soon longed for the creature comforts of the city and the warm enclosed quarters of the Motordrome.

The advanced training focused on fighting skills with emphasis placed on hand-to-hand combat, bayonet drills, and rifle range practice. To increase their stamina, the men embarked on lengthy route marches for hours and sometimes days across the rough terrain and hills of the camp. For the first time since Jean-Pierre's enlistment, manoeuvres included live ammunition. He crawled in the dirt and mud through obstacle courses as bullets cracked over his head and explosions shook the ground beneath him. His platoon attacked enemy positions with suppressing fire from machine guns to cover their advance. They used bangalore torpedoes to blow gaps in barbed wire, and grenades, guns and bayonets to finish the assault. Their training scope soon expanded from attacks with a platoon of 27 men to assaults with a company of 150 men and to manoeuvres involving soldiers, tanks, and artillery of the Fifth Brigade. Jean-Pierre marvelled at the commanders' abilities to manage the thousands of troops and their equipment. After three weeks, the black flies, drill instructors' abuse, bullets, and explosions no longer bothered Jean-Pierre. At day's end, he slept soundly. He felt physically and mentally ready for any challenge or task assigned to him.

In the camp, word filtered down to the troops of the near disaster in France. Almost 350,000 soldiers of the British Expeditionary Force and remnants of defeated French and Belgium armies trapped with their backs to the sea had been in danger of capture or annihilation by the approaching German armies. Only a miraculous escape back to England from the port of Dunkirk had saved the battle-hardened core of the British Army. Now the Germans stood poised, ready to attack England with only the English Channel in their way.

"It won't be long before we're shipped out," said a Fusilier sitting at a long table in the mess tent.

"Where do you think they'll send us?" asked the soldier sitting opposite him.

"Where else but England?"

"I bet we're going to France," mumbled another Fusilier through a mouthful of food. "It only makes sense for a French-speaking regiment to be sent there. Once we're through with the Germans we'll have some fun with the mademoiselles de Paris."

The Fusiliers' officers realised the call to battle might come sooner than expected and neither they nor their troops were ready. Training intensified and on 18 June 1940, the Fusiliers' commander received orders to prepare the Regiment for departure. News travelled through the ranks generating rumours and excitement among the eager young soldiers.

On 22 June, after almost four weeks of endless training and little rest, the soldiers went on 48-hours leave. Jean-Pierre and Maurice boarded a train to Montréal.

"Jean-Pierre, you need to find yourself a girl. After the war, I'm going to marry Pierrette and we're going to raise a family."

"You might be looking too far in the future, Maurice. They're not going to train us forever. They haven't given us leave because they want us to rest. They're going to send us somewhere."

"I know, but I'll have something to look forward to when it's all over. That's what you need too, my friend."

When they got off the train at the Bonaventure station, Maurice gave Jean-Pierre a brotherly hug. "See you in couple of days. If you find yourself with nothing to do, come out to Saint-Vincent-de-Paul. My mom would love to hear you sing."

"I've got to see my parents and sisters, which won't leave me with much time. Thanks anyway. Say hello to Pierrette and your parents for me."

While the men said their farewells to their loved ones, Germany formally concluded its sweep of the western European continent by accepting France's surrender. Hitler humiliated the French by conducting the surrender ceremony in the same place, in the same manner, and in the same railway carriage used by French Marshal Foch in 1918 when the Germans surrendered.

Jean-Pierre and Maurice returned to Valcartier on 24 June. Four days later, the soldiers underwent a screening for venereal diseases then packed their gear. For security purposes, the regiment shut down all means of contact with the outside world, preventing personnel from advising next of kin and friends of their imminent departure. On 29 June 1940, Private Jean-Pierre Laekas and his Regiment boarded a troop train, their destination known only by their officers.

Camp Valcartier, Québec 1940. Officers of Les Fusiliers Mont-Royal. From left to right: Erskine Eaton, Paul Trudeau, Jean Vézina and Yves Bourassa. *Courtesy of http://lesfusiliersmont-royal.com/*

Chapter 3
Empress of Australia
30 June 1940–7 July 1940

Twenty-four hours after leaving Valcartier, the train stopped alongside the docks at the port of Halifax, Nova Scotia. The men disembarked from the cars, assembled, and marched towards the red brick terminal building identified in big, bold letters as PIER 21. The Fusiliers joined the long column of troops already waiting to enter.

"Name and identification number," said the Regimental Company clerk standing at the entrance.

"Laekas, Jean-Pierre. D61894."

The clerk checked the list then put a tick beside his name. Jean-Pierre followed the line of soldiers exiting the rear of the building. With his kit bag slung over his shoulder, he walked up a metal ramp into the hull of a large ship.

As a Canadian Pacific passenger-liner, the Empress of Australia carried 1,500 customers in luxurious accommodations across the North Atlantic. In her new role as a troopship, the Empress accommodated thousands more. Dull-grey paint covered her Canadian Pacific colours of white and yellow and a three-inch gun stood on the promenade deck.

The Empress sailed out of Halifax harbour carrying the Cameron Highlanders of Ottawa and Les Fusiliers Mont-Royal. Most of the soldiers, including Jean-Pierre, had never been on a ship before. They gathered on every available open deck, leaning over the railings, and waving to no one in particular. While the tugboats escorted the Empress through the gap in the antisubmarine nets, Jean-Pierre looked back towards the city. The Citadel and the historic Old Town Clock stood majestically on the horizon. Destroyers, corvettes, and other warships crowded the harbour. As the Empress approached McNabs Island, the heavy cruiser HMS Devonshire joined them.

Once the Empress cleared the port of Halifax and reached open water, Jean-Pierre, Maurice, and the rest of "A" Company gathered for a briefing.

"We're part of a group called Z Force and we, together with the Cameron Highlanders, will join our sister regiment the Royals in Iceland," said the officer reading from a typed sheet.

Murmurs ran through the group as the men questioned their destination.

"Knock it off!" continued the officer. "You heard right. We're going to Iceland. Our job is to assist British regiments already there to defend the country from German invasion. Iceland is a guardian state of Denmark and as you know, the Germans occupied Denmark in April. To prevent the Germans from establishing a base in the North Atlantic with easier access to convoys heading to England, the British occupied Iceland in May."

"But sir, didn't Iceland declare its neutrality once Denmark surrendered to the Germans?" asked a politically astute Fusilier.

"A good question and it brings me to my next point," said the officer mentally taking note of the soldier who posed the query. "Following the arrival of the Brits, the Icelandic government issued a formal protest, insisting Britain respect their neutral status, which of course they didn't. Eventually, Iceland's Prime Minister told the population to consider the British soldiers as their guests and to treat them accordingly. Even with the government's support, there may be some Icelanders who won't appreciate our presence in their country. In all cases, you'll treat the Icelander's with respect and avoid situations which might result in conflict." The officer folded the typed transcript. "I don't want to hear of any of you upsetting the applecart by getting involved in fights with the men or socializing with the women. Remember, we're on our way to Iceland not as invaders but to help defend them from an invasion by the Germans."

The next morning at breakfast, Jean-Pierre met up with his friend Maurice.

"This is much better than Valcartier. I can't believe we're being served by waiters," said Jean-Pierre as he finished a mouthful of scrambled eggs.

"Did you know these waiters also served the British Royal Family?"

"What do you mean?"

"An officer told me the Royal family travelled to Canada on this ship. He said to enjoy the royal treatment while it lasts because Iceland is going to be much different."

"What's your cabin like?"

"Jean-Pierre, I'm not going to be cooped up in a cabin. I slept on deck near the middle funnel. I was very comfortable. You should join me. The fresh air will do you good."

"No thanks. I had enough fresh air at Valcartier to last a lifetime."

That evening Jean-Pierre stood on the main deck looking over the railing. He was mesmerised by the ship's hull cutting through the deep, grey water and the foam-capped waves drifting away from the ship. In the fading light, the distant horizon became a faint line as the dark water melded with the purple black sky. There was no sign of the Devonshire. No land, no other ships, they were alone. Nothing to protect them other than the three-inch gun on deck. *I wonder if there are any German submarines patrolling where we're headed.* He shivered at the thought then retired to the cabin he shared with three other Fusiliers.

Personnel of the 2nd Canadian Division, C.A.S.F., preparing to embark in troopship, Halifax, N.S., 1940. Canada. *Dept. Of National Defence / Library and Archives Canada / PA-114799/Other accession no.Ɪ1970-170 NPC.*

Canadian soldiers of the 2nd Canadian Division boarding ship to go overseas. *Canadian War Museum, Photo Archives 52A 4 18, 20020045-1909, DND Army WRA-419.*

Personnel of Les Fusiliers Mont-Royal and the Cameron Highlanders of Ottawa aboard the "H.M.T. Empress of Australia", Halifax, N.S., July 1940. Canada. *Dept. of National Defence / Library and Archives Canada / PA-114804.*

Troops of the 2nd Canadian Division leaving Halifax, 1940. *Canadian War Museum, Photo Archives 52A 4 18, 20020045-1910, NA- WRA-326.*

The Empress of Australia, 1940. *Private Collection.*

Chapter 4
Iceland
July 1940–October 1940

On 7 July 1940, Iceland's dark mountains and featureless shoreline appeared in the distance. Excited soldiers crowded the upper decks to watch the ship's approach to Reykjavík harbour. The Empress of Australia entered Faxaflói Bay then headed to its southern shore. As the ship approached the harbour, Jean-Pierre surveyed the countryside. *How odd. Where are the trees? Why is the ground so dark?* With the help of tugboats, the Empress edged towards the pier. Local stevedores caught and secured the ship's mooring lines.

"First platoon, "A" Company! Lead off!" shouted the sergeant major.

Jean-Pierre walked down the gangplank and stepped onto the pier. *Well, they promised me travel and adventure. Here I am in Iceland. I wonder when the adventure begins.*

The regiments marched from the port to an open area outside the town. The sight of 2,000 Canadian soldiers winding their way through the streets of Reykjavík to the skirl of the Cameron Highlanders of Ottawa's bagpipes made quite an impression on the locals. By late afternoon, the soldiers had erected their tent city and relaxed, enjoying the summer weather. That evening, when the bugler played taps, some men retired to their tents while others continued whatever they were doing.

"Soldiers, lights out means it's time to break up the game," said an officer passing by Jean-Pierre and a group of Fusiliers playing cards.

"Sir, the sun is still up."

"That's right, Private. This is Iceland and unlike you, the sun never sleeps. Now put the cards away."

On 11 July, "A" Company received orders to set up a permanent camp in Hveragerði, 60 miles southeast of Reykjavík. Jean-Pierre packed his gear then joined his platoon in formation. They marched through the countryside, surrounded by a desolate black landscape dotted with spots of green where moss and lichen grew. There were no trees, bushes, shrubs, or flowers. In the distance, brooding, black mountains rose high into the clear blue sky.

"The black ground is lava. It flowed centuries ago," said the Fusilier marching beside Jean-Pierre. "Iceland was born from volcanoes and some are still active, perhaps even those." He nodded his head towards the mountains. Pointing at a distant geyser, he continued with his documentary. "And over there you can see the steam rising from the hillside. The lava below the ground is heating water and causing steam to rise to the surface."

"So why do they call it Iceland?"

"Apparently the Vikings who discovered the island were enamoured with its raw beauty. To discourage others from coming, they called it Iceland."

"And I suppose you're going to tell me they called Greenland by that name to attract other Vikings."

"You've got it!"

The gradually ascending road climbed to the crest of a high plain. Nestled in the valley below, was a small town, their destination of Hveragerði. The long column of soldiers snaked down the steep switchback road to the open fields outside the town where they set up their tents. The next day, the Regiment assembled for a formal ceremony to replace the incumbent British 49th Infantry Division Lancashire Fusiliers.

"Hey, mates!" yelled a British soldier after the ceremony. "Build up a peat berm against the sides of your tent facing the bloody prevailing wind. This is a miserable place but it's even worse when the wind and the rain get into your tents."

What the hell is he talking about? thought Jean-Pierre.

Once the men settled in, an officer assembled them for a briefing.

"The Brits need a couple of runways so they can bring in fighters and coastal command planes. Our job is to build them," said the briefing officer. "Over there at Kaldaðarnes."

The men turned their heads in the direction the officer pointed. Flat open fields lay between their tented camp and a large winding river. On the other side of the river appeared to be farmers' fields.

"Each Company will work in shifts of one week. We'll start with "A" Company and go through sequentially to "F" Company until we're done. Because of the distance, the Company working at Kaldaðarnes will camp there for the week."

"Sir, how long will it take?" asked a Fusilier.

"The engineer in charge says it'll take six months. We need to remove a lava hill and level the lava plain. It'll be hard work but I'm confident Les Fusiliers will rise to the occasion. I told the engineer the runways would be ready well ahead of his six-month estimate. I don't expect you men are going to make a liar out of me by taking six months to finish the runways, are you?"

The men laughed and cheered, eager to take up the challenge. The next morning, trucks transported Jean-Pierre, Maurice, and the rest of "A" Company to Kaldaðarnes. They crossed the Ölfus River at Selfoss then several miles later turned onto a small road. After a short distance, it became a rutted bumpy track leading them through farm fields. After a rough ride, they arrived at a large open field alongside the water. Jean-Pierre could see the town of Hveragerði, miles away on the other side of the Ölfus River. Once the men set up their tents on the riverbanks, they gathered around for another briefing of the project by the British Military Engineering officer in charge.

"Your task is to construct a runway defined by the stakes I've placed in the ground."

Jean-Pierre looked in the direction the soldier pointed. Two parallel lines of evenly spaced wooden pegs marked the runway's outline through a field of untended straw-coloured grass. The pegs followed the contour of the field's mounds and depressions.

"The ground beneath the vegetation is lava. Your job is to level the area for the runway, taxiway, and aprons. Your tools will be picks, shovels, wheelbarrows, and dynamite."

The word dynamite sent an excited chatter through the assembled young men.

"The dynamite is for the large elongated hill over there. I estimate it'll take six months to finish the runway but your officer told me it would be done sooner. We'll see."

The work commenced with most men drawing picks and shovels while a smaller group selected by "A" Company's sergeant including Jean-Pierre and Maurice joined the engineer at the lava hill.

"We insert the sticks of dynamite into holes that you'll make in the lava. I'll show you."

The engineer took three dynamite sticks then climbed up the hill. He placed each stick in a prepared hole then unrolled the dynamite's wires as he backed down the hill. After securing the wires to the detonator terminals, he pulled a whistle from his pocket and blew three shrill blasts. He looked towards the hill and once satisfied the site was clear, he thrust down the detonator's plunger. A second later, the ground shuddered and from the side of the hill, chunks of black lava, smoke, and dust flew in the air.

The men joined the engineer as he walked up the hill.

"The next step is to remove the rubble then blow up some more of this hill. Are there any questions?"

Silence followed as the men realised the magnitude of their task.

"Fine then, I'll leave you to your work."

Despite a cool breeze coming off the nearby river, the men sweated profusely as they used their picks and shovels to clear the area.

"This is going to take a hell of a long time," said Maurice watching Jean-Pierre carry a large piece of the black volcanic emission. "I'm going to ask the sergeant if we can use more dynamite, otherwise this *will* take six months."

The sergeant, unimpressed by the effects of the three-stick explosion, agreed with Maurice's suggestion. Following the sergeant's instructions, the men prepared for the next blast. They inserted multiple sticks of primed dynamite in each hole and ran the wires back to the detonator. Once satisfied all was ready, the sergeant gave the signal. Maurice shoved the plunger down. A large segment of the hill leaped skyward and the ground trembled beneath their feet. As pieces of lava rock rained down near them, the sound of the explosion echoed off the mountains behind Hveragerði. The men of "A" Company rushed through a cloud of dust and smoke to inspect the results of their handiwork. The explosion had removed a large portion of the hill. Clumps of black lava rock ranging from fist-sized pieces to large boulders lay scattered about the base of the slope. The men cheered, laughed, and congratulated each other on their success.

"Come on boys. Let's get going. Clean up the debris and we'll take another piece out of this bloody hill," said the sergeant.

The men with picks and shovels set to work removing the rubble while Maurice, Jean-Pierre, and the rest of the explosives' team prepared new holes for their dynamite. At the end of the first week, the fatigued but satisfied men of "A" Company turned their tools and newly acquired terrain-levelling knowledge over to "B" Company and returned to Hveragerði.

Much to the dismay of the soldiers, the unseasonably warm weather ended. Periods of rain came in the form of sudden squalls or drenching downpours. One night, Jean-Pierre woke with a start. The sides of his tent flapped uncontrollably in the wind and a drop of water hit his forehead. As he wondered about the source, several other drops hit him.

"Shit!" he exclaimed. He threw back the covers and in the dim light, peered at the water dripping from a saturated seam. He moved his bed and tried to get back to sleep. *What did that Brit say about the bloody wind and rain?*

In his spare time, Jean-Pierre played cards, read, played cards, learned some Icelandic expressions, played cards, and wrote letters to his parents and sisters. He visited the town of Hveragerði whenever he had leave and discovered the dwellings on the island relied on subterranean hot water as their source of heat. After several weeks of the camp's daily diet of mutton, Jean-Pierre looked for every opportunity to avoid the fried or roasted meat served by the Regiment's chef. He ate in the town or bought sandwiches from the local entrepreneurs who set up stands near the camp. The Icelanders resented the British and Canadian armies' presence, but they soon warmed to the *bon vivant* nature of the Fusiliers. Jean-Pierre and Maurice ignored the non-fraternisation orders taking every opportunity to socialise with the friendly, blue-eyed, blonde-haired Icelandic women.

The continual bleating of sheep from nearby farms coupled with the midnight sun deprived Jean-Pierre of sleep. Iceland's novelty began to wane. He felt damp and chilled even on clear days. The army-issued wood stoves stood useless outside his tent, because looking for wood was a futile exercise on the treeless landscape. Garrison duty in Hveragerði replaced Jean-Pierre's less formal camp life at Kaldaðarnes where he enjoyed blowing up lava hills and fishing in the Ölfus River. Some days he performed guard duty on the base or in the town. Other days he went on long foot patrols along the coast, searching for German soldiers who might have landed from U Boats lurking offshore in Iceland's many bays and fjords.

Six weeks after work commenced, RAF Kaldaðarnes stood ready to receive its first aircraft. A useable runway of crushed lava stone stood in place of the site's former lava hill and uneven lava plain.

On 27 August, nine RAF Fairey Battle aircraft of RAF No. 98 Squadron landed. That night the proud Fusiliers celebrated their achievement, four months ahead of schedule.

The Regiment's Companies continued to work on the small airport's network of roads and anti-aircraft posts, and stood guard over the RAF fighter-bombers. Another nine aircraft arrived in September to join the coastal patrols and pursuit of submarines in the waters around Iceland.

The arrival of aviation fuel for the aircraft provided Jean-Pierre and his regiment with some relief from the cold and damp. Using the airport's large supply of discarded five-gallon drums, the Fusiliers made stoves. They removed the top, filled the bottom of the drum with six inches of sand and crushed lava stone then poured in aviation fuel. Singed eyebrows and soot-blackened faces marked those who used too much fuel or stood too close when they threw the lit match into the drum.

One night, a young Fusilier named Arthur Fraser patrolled the airfield, guarding the planes. Intrigued by the fighter-bombers, he inspected one carefully, looking at the aircraft's markings. He had never been on a plane or seen one up close. Arthur looked around. Confident he was alone, he removed his bayonet and scribed his name and birth date on the plane's wing. The next day, the Company commander summoned Arthur to his tent.

"Private Fraser, what possessed you to put your bloody name on a plane's wing."

"Sir, yesterday was my 18th birthday."

"I don't give a shit if it was your mother's 100th birthday. You've damaged a very expensive aircraft. I'm putting you on report."

The officer rose from his desk and approached Arthur who still stood at attention.

"Private, did you shave this morning?" he said peering through his glasses at the few blond wisps of hair on Arthur's young chin." Before Arthur could respond, the officer thundered, "What bloody insubordination! First the plane, now this. I'm docking you a day's wages. Now get the hell out of here."

Arthur snapped a salute, did a smart about face, and marched out of the tent.

With the European continent secured, Germany now prepared for the invasion of England. The Canadian Parliament responded to Britain's request for troops and approved the proposal to send the Second Canadian Division to England. In recognition of their service in Iceland, the Canadian Regiments proudly wore a distinctive patch on their uniform of a white polar bear on a black background.

On 31 October 1940, after four months in Iceland, Les Fusiliers Mont-Royal left Hveragerði for Reykjavík harbour. The Royal Regiment of Canada joined Les Fusiliers while the Cameron Highlanders of Ottawa remained destined to spend the winter on the cold, desolate island.

In high spirits, Jean-Pierre helped his mates unload the transport trucks at the harbour, pleased to leave behind the stark, barren country. During his four-month stay, he laboured more than he soldiered and swung a pick more often than he carried his rifle. His living quarters were primitive. Most nights he slept cold and damp in his uniform and rose the same way. He hated the dreadful mutton. Despite the adversities, Jean-Pierre recognized the changes brought about by his Regiment's stay on the island. The soldiers learned to adapt to the harsh conditions and depend on each other. The experience bonded them in a way their training in Montréal and Valcartier could not. They shared common hardships, sacrifices, and achievements. They had departed Halifax as a group of raw recruits, loosely bound by regional borders and their French Canadian mother tongue. Now they were going to England as a tightly knit unit ready to fight the enemy.

Personnel of Les Fusiliers Mont-Royal, Reykjavik, Iceland, 1940. *Canadian War Museum, 19920085-1121.*

Personnel of Les Fusiliers Mont-Royal manning machine-gun, Iceland, 1940. *Canadian War Museum, 19920085-1122.*

Personnel of Les Fusiliers Mont-Royal, Iceland, 1940. *Canadian War Museum, 19920085-1114.*

Tents of Les Fusiliers Mont-Royal, Iceland, 1940. *Canadian War Museum, 19920085-1115.*

Personnel of Les Fusiliers Mont-Royal, Iceland, 1940. *Canadian War Museum, 19920085-1116.*

Tents of Les Fusiliers Mont-Royal, Iceland, 1940. *Canadian War Museum, 19920085-1117*

Mail call, Iceland, 1940. *Courtesy of http://www.camerons.ca/Album_WWII.html*

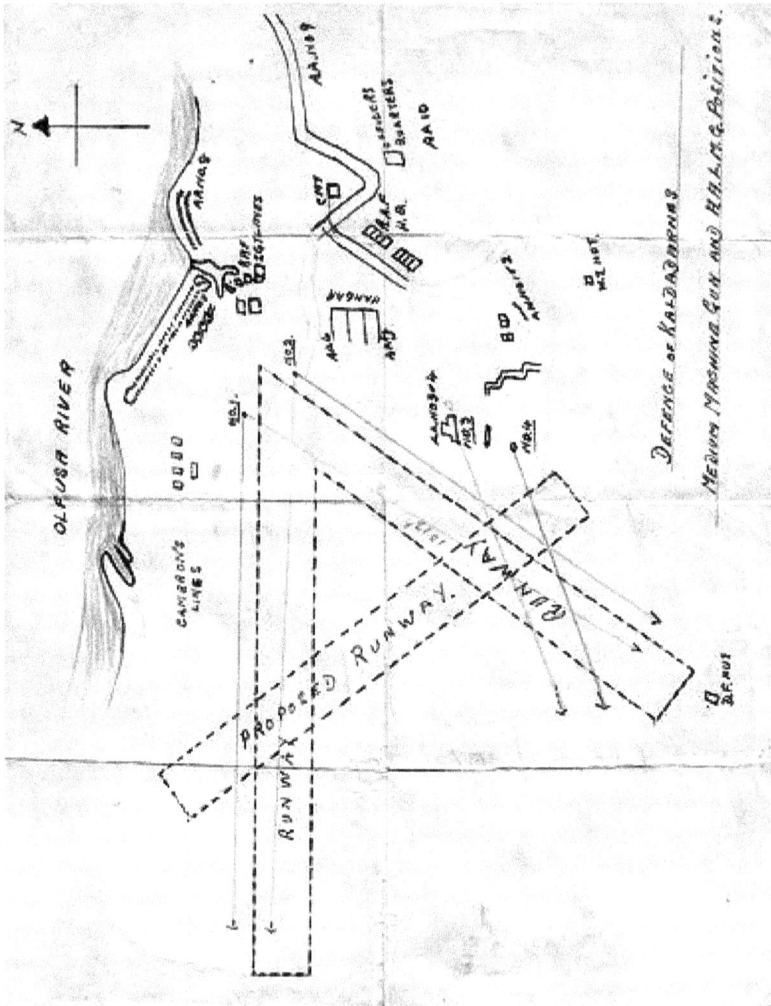

A sketch map of the medium and light machine gun defensive positions of the 1st Battalion, The Cameron Highlanders of Ottawa (M.G.), C.A.S.F., at the Kaldadarnes airfield near Reykjavik, Iceland, in 1940 and 1941. *Courtesy of http://www.camerons.ca/*

Chapter 5
S.S. Antonia
31 October 1940–3 November 1940

The 1,800 soldiers of the Royal Regiment of Canada and Les Fusiliers Mont-Royal gathered at the docks in Reykjavík harbour anticipating a lengthy boarding process. To pass the time, they talked about where they had been, where they were going, and the ship that would take them there.

"I doubt that we'll be served by the waiters who looked after the Royal family, like on the Empress," said a Fusilier.

"Don't worry. There are no bloody waiters on this one," replied a sailor passing by.

Formerly, a passenger ship of the Cunard White Star line, the British Navy chartered the S.S. Antonia at the outbreak of the war to serve as a troopship. The ship's armament included four 4-inch guns as well as eight 40 mm and 20 mm anti-aircraft guns.

Once aboard, Jean-Pierre and Maurice jostled their way past other soldiers below decks to find their assigned quarters. The ship's public rooms, social halls, and all other open areas including the ship's holds were fitted with row upon row of multi-tiered bunks.

"I won't be sleeping down here," said Maurice frowning. "I'll be somewhere on deck out in the open air. Why don't you join me?"

"You're crazy Maurice. It's the end of October. Once the wind and the cold get to you, you'll come crawling back inside."

They threw their helmets, gas masks, and haversacks on the bunks then climbed to the upper deck.

"You see the pom-pom over there," said Maurice pointing to the multi-barrelled 40 mm gun station near the ship's bow. "That's where you'll find me. I'm going to get assigned as a gunner for the trip."

"Good luck. I'll save you a place below deck just in case."

"Perhaps I'd better save a spot for you when you come crawling up here for air," he countered.

Days later, after all troops and equipment were loaded, Jean-Pierre felt the rumble below decks as the S.S. Antonia's steam turbines responded to the signals from the ship's bridge. Dockworkers cast off the ship's bow and stern mooring lines from the pier, then waved to the troops lining the decks as the S.S. Antonia slipped away from her berth. They departed as part of a convoy that included their old friend the Empress of Australia. Jean-Pierre watched the receding coastline and marvelled at the raw beauty of the dark rugged hills and the cloud-capped mountains. *A beautiful place but thank God we're leaving.*

At nightfall, most men retreated to their berths below, but a few stayed on deck, including Maurice. Wearing his helmet and all the cold weather clothes he possessed, he settled into the gunner's seat behind the 40 mm guns in the bow. He placed a large supply of saltines in a secure area next to his canteen full of water, fastened the harness, and closed his eyes, content with his choice of accommodations.

Once the S.S. Antonia reached the open seas, the wind picked up and the ocean's gentle swells became towering walls of water. The ship climbed the huge waves, balanced briefly at their crests and rocked from side to side before plunging down their backsides to meet another approaching wall of water. The sea burst over the bow, flooding the deck and washing loose items over the sides. Maurice, tightly secured in his harness, sat hunched behind the guns, seeking what little protection his station offered from the elements.

When the storm passed, Jean-Pierre ventured top side to escape the lingering smell of vomit permeating the decks below. He found Maurice still sitting at the anti-aircraft gun station.

"I told you it would be better on deck," said Maurice when he saw his friend's sallow face. "Fresh air, saltines, and water are all you need."

At the mention of food, Jean-Pierre's queasiness returned. He clamped his hand over his mouth and ran for the railing.

The S.S. Antonia left the turbulent North Atlantic Ocean and entered the Inner Seas off Scotland's west coast, shadowed by a

Sunderland Flying Boat from RAF 246 Squadron based at the nearby Isle of Islay. They approached the Irish Sea's North Channel, a narrow 10-mile gap between Ireland and Scotland. Jean-Pierre stayed on deck, the fresh air providing some relief from his earlier discomfort. He noticed the ship's lookouts scanning the horizon and realised danger still lurked out in the open water and skies.

"Have you spotted any Germans yet?" asked Jean-Pierre.

"Not yet," responded the sailor, "but they're out there. A few weeks ago some U Boats and Focke-Wulf Condor bombers sank some ships not too far from here."

The S.S. Antonia sailed through the Channel without incident then turned in to the Firth of Clyde. A Fusilier familiar with Scotland's history and geography pointed out some of the sights they passed.

"The island in the distance is Ailsa Craig. The granite from its quarries is used to make curling stones."

"Didn't know they curled hair with stones," another soldier quipped, drawing some laughs and a few puzzled looks.

Fascinated by the beautiful Scottish coastline, Jean-Pierre borrowed a pair of binoculars from a sailor no longer on lookout duty. Magnificent centuries-old castles, small villages, and golf courses appeared in his lenses as they sailed past the towns of Ayr, Prestwick, and Troon.

The S.S. Antonia entered the Firth of Clyde leading to the port of Gourock, passing Little Cumbrae and Great Cumbrae, the two islands guarding the channel entrance. Soldiers lined the decks anxious to set foot on dry land. Once past the town of Dunoon, a sturdy little tugboat guided them. The soldiers stared in awe at the sheer number of transport and naval vessels anchored in the harbour.

"Looks like there's a war going on," joked a Fusilier.

On 3 November 1940, the S.S. Antonia docked at the port of Gourock, Scotland. Most soldiers walked down the gangplank on unsteady legs and with empty stomachs, eager to put this part of the journey behind them. However, Maurice disembarked looking no worse for wear and feeling proud of his ability to have endured the crossing that gave much grief to his mates.

From the port, the Regiments marched to the nearby Gourock train station. In the early evening, they boarded a troop train destined for Aldershot, 500 miles away in the south of England.

S.S. Antonia. *Private Collection.*

Port of Gourock, Scotland, during WWII. *Courtesy of the Gourock Library.*

Chapter 6
Aldershot, England
November 1940–December 1940

Jean-Pierre and Maurice stared out the train's windows at the lush Scottish countryside. The rolling hills, trees, and villages with quaint stone cottages contrasted starkly to the barren landscape of Iceland.

"When we get leave I'd like to come back to this area. It reminds me of home," said Maurice.

They passed through Glasgow, a large, sprawling city with neatly arranged blocks of houses, factories, parks, and shopping districts. The setting of the sun and the train's rocking motion soon put most of the weary soldiers to sleep. The train travelled through the night with occasional stops on sidings to allow northbound trains to pass. The next day, with seven hours left in their journey, the men kept busy by chatting, playing cards, eating, and watching the countryside roll by.

They arrived at the town of Aldershot in the afternoon of 4 November 1940. From the train station they marched a short distance to the sprawling military garrison. Les Fusiliers set about finding their bunks and storing their gear in the Talavera barracks. Constructed in 1859, the barracks housing the Canadians consisted of two tired, three-storey buildings in need of a good cleaning and fresh coat of paint. There were 10 rooms on each floor and each room held 25 men. Dim lighting and a small coal fireplace added to the depressing appearance and the dampness of the rooms.

"Christ," said Maurice. "These barracks are ancient."

"They're still a hell of a lot better than our tents in Iceland," replied Jean-Pierre.

That night as Jean-Pierre lay in his bunk, for the first time since leaving Montréal, he heard air raid sirens and the distant sound of bombing. *This is the real thing*, he thought. Thankful he had a roof over his head and the bed was not rocking, he fell into a deep sleep.

The next day, the regiment turned out for drills and marching. The size of the camp with its barracks, mess halls, parade grounds, and expanse of other military buildings impressed the Canadians. The garrison, home to over 100,000 British and Commonwealth soldiers, consisted of more than 35 separate barracks.

Les Fusiliers had no time for rest. Training exercises, mock battles, and manoeuvres against British troops filled their days. During an exercise, Maurice prepared for an ambush of the British by hiding in the branches of a large tree extending over a narrow road. As the enemy vehicles passed beneath him, he dropped a non-lethal training grenade into a jeep carrying an officer. The grenade exploded with a thunderous bang wounding the British officer's pride.

Maurice's antics against the British continued. During a night manoeuvre, he discovered the location of a British unit's provisions. The Canadians stole a truck and used it to pilfer the British unit's supplies. The next morning, when the angry Brits discovered the missing food including their beloved tea, they called in an umpire. The umpire and a British officer from the victimised unit arrived at the Fusiliers' camp shortly after dawn.

"What the bloody hell do you think you're doing?" bellowed the umpire at Maurice and the other offenders. "You don't bloody well steal another unit's provisions."

The men played dumb and responded in French, pleading their innocence.

"Bloody undisciplined, unsportsmanlike colonials," muttered the officer. "Get those damn supplies back right now or you'll all be up on charges."

Maurice and his friends chuckled as the furious officer stormed off, leaving the umpire to deal with the Fusiliers.

Aldershot provided plenty of attractions to keep the men occupied during their leisure time, including sports fields, cinemas, canteens, shops, pubs, libraries, and plenty of women. It did not take long for the Canadians to take over the town and develop close friendships with the townsfolk.

The Fusiliers received 10 days Landing and Privilege leave on 19 November. Despite the allure of England, Jean-Pierre and Maurice decided to return to Scotland. They packed their kits, signed out of the barracks, then walked to the nearby train station joining other members of their Regiment taking leave. They met Arthur who was going to Inverness. In a card game a few days earlier, Arthur lost all his pay and could not afford to go on leave. The winner of the card game offered to pay Arthur's way to Inverness if he agreed to be his batman. Forever the opportunist, Arthur refused to let his pride get in the way of a chance to leave the base so he agreed to be the personal servant of the soldier.

"Hey Arthur," called a Fusilier watching him struggle with two kit bags. "When you're done putting those on the train, could you be a good lad and do mine?"

"For five pounds, I'll do that and shine your boots," replied Arthur.

"You know what? The bugger will probably do it," said the Fusilier as the group continued to watch Arthur.

Two hours later in London, Jean-Pierre and Maurice changed trains at the Kings Cross station. The train to Glasgow carried a mix of civilians and military personnel and stopped a number of times along the route. At one station, a few young girls boarded and sat opposite the soldiers.

"Good morning young ladies. My name is Maurice. How are you?"

The girls giggled. "What a lovely accent. Where are you from?" asked one of the girls.

"We're French-Canadian sent to England to protect you from a German invasion," said Jean-Pierre smiling before Maurice could respond. "My name is Jean-Pierre."

Captivated by the handsome young foreigners in uniform, the girls laughed and flirted with the two Fusiliers until the train reached the young women's destination. As the train pulled out of the station, the men waved goodbye then settled back in their seats to discuss the girls' physical attributes. Once their excitement passed, Maurice fell asleep while Jean-Pierre gazed with unseeing eyes out the window. *Was it only six months ago that I was in Montréal working at my uncle's garage? Valcartier, Iceland, England, and now I'm in Scotland 3,000 miles away from home.* He shook his head in amazement thinking about the route on which fate had taken him. *Where will it end?*

In Glasgow, they found a room at the YMCA. They flopped on their beds, feeling strangely tired from the day's inactivity. The next day after touring the city, they returned to the Y. They relaxed in the lounge and Maurice practised his English by reading articles to Jean-Pierre from the Glasgow Herald.

"Did you find that interesting?" said a young girl seated nearby.

"Pardon?" said Jean-Pierre turning to the girl. Her long brown hair framed a pretty, oval face.

"What your friend just read about the German spies in England."

"I suppose. But he's only reading it to practise his English and I'm helping him."

"What language does he normally speak?"

"French. We're from Montréal, a city in Canada, and it's mostly French there. My name is Jean-Pierre and this is Maurice." Maurice nodded his head.

"Well how do you do. I'm Margaret and here comes my sister Kathy."

A pretty, young girl with short curly hair approached.

"Kathy, this is Jean-Pierre and Maurice from Canada," she said. "Maurice was having English lessons when I rudely interrupted him." Maurice and Jean-Pierre laughed.

"Would you like to join us? We're going to get something to eat," said Jean-Pierre.

"Luv to," replied Kathy without hesitation.

The girls led them to a small pub where they spent the rest of the afternoon chatting.

"Would you like to go to the dance tonight at the Y?" asked Margaret as they   prepared to leave.

"Luv to," replied Maurice imitating Kathy.

That night when the dance finished, the girls insisted the men give up their rooms at the YMCA and stay at their parent's boarding house where they would be more comfortable. The men agreed, gathered their haversacks, and checked out of the YMCA. Strolling through town, Jean-Pierre chatted away with the girls while Maurice tried to keep up with the conversation. A few blocks later, they arrived at 40 Argyle Street near the River Clyde.

"Wonderful," said Mrs. Lyon after Margaret told her mother the story. "We can't have you staying at the Y, now can we? There's plenty of room here. We'll have you fixed up in a jiffy."

"Well now, who do we have here?" said Mr. Lyon in a booming voice when he arrived home later that evening. "Looks like we've been invaded by Canadians, if I'm not mistaken."

A veteran of the First War, Mr. Lyon worked as a police officer in the city of Glasgow and was familiar with the uniforms of the Commonwealth armies from encounters with boisterous and unruly soldiers.

"These young men will be boarding with us, my dear."

"Brilliant," responded Mr. Lyon. "Where are you chaps based?"

"Aldershot," replied Jean-Pierre.

"Let these lads have a bite before you ask anymore questions," said Mrs. Lyon.

Between spoonfuls of hearty chicken soup, Jean-Pierre explained the journey that brought them to Glasgow, including the resemblance of Scotland's beautiful countryside to the rugged area north of Montréal.

"No doubt you've noticed Scotland's other beautiful resources," responded Mr. Lyon with a twinkle in his eye.

Mr. Lyon burst out laughing at Jean-Pierre's puzzled expression.

"My boy, you must have noticed the pretty girls all about, including the two seated here." He laughed as his daughters protested their father's bold comment.

After they finished eating, Mr. Lyon led them to the lounge. "Boys, have you ever had Laphroaig Single Malt Scotch Whisky?"

"No, sir," they said in unison shaking their heads.

"Well this wonderful elixir comes from the Laphroaig Distillery in Port Ellen on the Isle of Islay," he explained in a reverent tone.

"Didn't we pass the Isle of Islay as we approached Scotland?" asked Jean-Pierre.

"Aye, that you did." He poured three fingers of Scotch into a fine crystal glass.

After one drink, Jean-Pierre retired to bed. He slept so soundly he did not wake when Maurice stumbled to the room, many glasses later.

The men remained at the Lyon family's boarding house for the rest of their leave. Maurice visited nearby farms and towns with Margaret who found his French accent and broken English charming. Kathy adored Jean-Pierre and insisted on escorting him around Glasgow to see the sights. At night, they went to movies and dances. Though Jean-Pierre's footwork lacked subtleness, he had a very good ear for music and loved to sing. One evening when they were all in the Lyon's kitchen, Jean-Pierre started singing *Begin the Beguine*, one of his favourite songs. When he finished, the Lyons applauded while Maurice laughed at his friend's spontaneity. The rest of the evening became a songfest as they sang, laughed, and drank whisky.

After 10 days, Maurice and Jean-Pierre regretted leaving. With much hugging and kissing, the Lyon family said their goodbyes, insisting the two Fusiliers return on their next leave. To show their appreciation for their Scottish hosts' hospitality, they gave the Lyons their ration coupons for butter and eggs, cartons of cigarettes, and boxes of sugar cubes they carried in their haversacks.

When they arrived back at camp, their sergeant major told them to remove their Iceland service polar bear patch from their uniforms.

"Regimental Orders," he said seeing the bewildered looks on their faces. "For security reasons we have to replace it with a blue rectangle identifying our regiment as part of the Second Canadian Division."

"What's the security reason, Sergeant Major?" asked Jean-Pierre.

"The Brits don't want it known that we left Iceland. It's either because they think the Huns will realise Iceland is weaker because we left or England is now weaker because we're here." He laughed at his joke then walked away.

Some members of the Royal Regiment of Canada and Les Fusiliers refused to remove their patches. The revolt did not last long and the polar bear insignia soon disappeared from their uniforms.

Failing to defeat the RAF in the Battle of Britain in October, Germany's air force turned to sustained attacks on England's cities, ports, and industrial centres, trying to bomb the country in to submission. One day a distant droning rumble caught Arthur's attention as he passed through the camp entrance on his way to the barracks.

"What the hell is that?" he asked the guard at the gate.

"Just the regular visit by the Jerries. If you look to the west you can just about make them out."

Arthur looked in the direction the guard pointed and could see a cluster of dark specks in the pale blue sky.

"Are they coming here?"

"Unlikely. We had a single bomber come by a few weeks ago. He was probably lost. He shot up the camp, killed three of your chaps, and wounded about 30 others. Most likely they're headed for London."

As the German planes approached the camp, Arthur could make out their distinctive bubble-nose.

"They're Heinkel one elevens."

"Right you are."

The formation slowly veered away from Aldershot ignoring the sprawling military garrison. Later that day Arthur found out the German bombers attacked London and severely damaged the port area.

Not only did the Germans shower England with bombs, but they also made their presence known through their English-language propaganda radio program, *Germany Calling.* The program attempted to demoralize the British population and Commonwealth troops stationed in England through reports of Allied losses. In the barracks, Arthur listened regularly to the broadcasts, intrigued by the announcer's knowledge of local conditions.

"Jairmany   calling, Jairmany calling," said the English announcer in a distinct nasal drawl. Lord Haw Haw proceeded to report on the numbers of Allied casualties, downed aircraft, and ships lost to German action.

"Hello members of the Second Canadian Division in Aldershot," continued Lord Haw Haw.

Arthur jerked his head up as the announcer mentioned the name of his division.

"If you're planning on meeting your girl at the town clock, please note it's 15 minutes late."

Arthur's jaw dropped. *How did he know that?*

"The English could do us a great favour by giving all you brave young Canadians motorcycles," said Lord Haw Haw. "This would save us the cost of having to shoot you because we know you're killing yourselves driving on the English roads."

Arthur shook his head in disbelief. *How did he get all this information? Where is he and why is this bloody Limey working for the Germans?*

During his leisure time, Jean-Pierre spoke with several British soldiers who fought the Germans in France and North Africa. These discussions with seasoned veterans brought things in to perspective for Jean-Pierre. While he engaged in staged battles during exercises with his regiment, elsewhere young men like him fought and died in real battles. He admired the exploits and courage of the British veterans and longed for the opportunity to do the same.

Talavera barracks at Aldershot, England. *Courtesy of the Aldershot Military Museum.*

Interior of Talavera barracks. *Courtesy of Aldershot Military Museum.*

Jean-Pierre (far left), Kathy Lyon (second from left), Maurice (third from left), and other members of the Lyon family. Glasgow, Scotland. *Courtesy of Maurice Jolicoeur.*

Jean-Pierre (far right) with members of the Lyon family. Glasgow, Scotland. *Courtesy of Maurice Jolicoeur.*

Chapter 7
Cove, England
December 1940–June 1941

In late December, Les Fusiliers packed their gear and left for the barracks at Cove, eight miles northwest of Aldershot. Despite being much smaller than Aldershot, the camp easily accommodated the regiment. The men occupied the Guillemont Barracks, recently vacated by the Calgary Highlanders. A central heating system in the barracks provided a pleasant change from the damp and cold of Talavera.

Jean-Pierre received a 48-hour Christmas pass, insufficient time for a quick getaway to the Lyons so he decided to join a group of Fusiliers going to London. When he arrived in the city, the scale and intensity of destruction left Jean-Pierre stunned. The blackened skeletons of buildings gutted by fires stood in stark contrast to those left untouched. He walked by huge mounds of rubble where a home destroyed by a bomb's explosion once stood. He sidestepped deep craters in roads that exposed the shattered innards of the city's infrastructure of water mains, gas pipes, and electrical lines. Civilians, policemen, and military personnel all went about their business skirting the rubble in the streets, seemingly oblivious to the damage left by German bombers. That evening the shrill sound of air raid sirens sent him from the comfort of his bed to the nearest shelter.

While he trained in Canada, the distant war in Europe meant very little to him. He regarded the training he had in Montréal and Valcartier as extensions of war games he played as a youth. Iceland added a sense of realism because he was in a foreign land guarding seaports and cities. However, England turned his games in to reality with its nightly blackouts, bombed cities, and assembled armies of various nationalities.

The next day he returned to Cove with the dark images of London running through his mind, blocking out all thoughts of his first Christmas away from home.

The Fusiliers' training continued uninterrupted through England's damp winter. Rain or shine, every Sunday Jean-Pierre's Company marched eight miles to the rifle range at Aldershot for target practice then marched eight miles back to Cove. The season's frequent and chilling downpours left the men drenched, cold, and miserable. *This beats Iceland at its worst*, thought Jean-Pierre clutching his rifle in his numb hands as he pushed his way through the wet undergrowth in search of the enemy. Fortunately, the men had received a second battledress and another pair of boots enabling them to stay reasonably dry.

On 21 February 1941, Jean-Pierre left with Maurice for 9 days leave, their destination the Lyon family residence in Glasgow. Although three months had passed since their last visit, Mrs. Lyon greeted them warmly.

"What a delight," she said with a broad smile as she embraced them both. "Come in. You must be famished after your journey. I've got some lovely mutton Scotch pies I'm sure you'll enjoy."

As they followed Mrs. Lyon, Maurice and Jean-Pierre looked at each other and grimaced.

"Our favourite," exclaimed Jean-Pierre.

When the girls arrived, Margaret and Kathy hugged their dance partners with delight. Mr. Lyon insisted they have a glass of whisky before supper to celebrate the boys' return. Soon one became two and the evening meal developed in to a long drawn out affair with much laughter, singing, and more glasses of Laphroaig.

During their 9-day stay, Mr. Lyon took the boys to his favourite pub for a drink. Proud of his Canadians, he wanted to show them off to his friends. They played billiards and though a far more accomplished player than they, Mr. Lyon let them win a few games. They left the pub late in the evening with Jean-Pierre and Maurice propping Mr. Lyon up as they sang their way home.

Jean-Pierre went to dances and movies, and took long walks around Glasgow with Kathy. The days seemed to fly by. She was his first girlfriend and he wondered where their relationship would take them. Their leave ended all too soon and following the girls' teary goodbyes, Maurice and Jean-Pierre left to catch the train back to Cove. During the train ride, Jean-Pierre probed Maurice about his relationship with Margaret.

"Do you like her?"

"Of course I like her. Why do you ask?"

"You were the one who told me you were going to marry Pierrette and raise a family."

"That's right and I will. But you're the one who told me not to look too far in to the future." Maurice laughed pointing playfully at Jean-Pierre. "So while I'm here, I'm going to enjoy myself. When I get home, I'll tell my lovely Pierrette all about Margaret and any other girls we encounter. And what about you and Kathy?"

"Well I like her a lot but ..."

"But what?" interrupted Maurice impatient to hear his friend's disclosure.

"I'm not sure if I'm ready to make a commitment like you've made to Pierrette."

"Trust me, when the right one comes along, you'll know it."

The men returned to more training and miserable weather. At times, the rain drove down in sheets, flooding their trenches and soaking their equipment. The soldiers struggled in the mud and water towards their objectives wondering why anyone would want to fight in such miserable conditions.

On the morning of 25 March 1941, the Sergeant Major assembled "A" Company on the parade ground.

"Today there'll be no training."

The men remained silent not knowing what to expect.

"Instead you will prepare for an inspection at 1100 hours. I want to see my reflection in your boots and brass buttons and the crease in your uniforms as sharp as razors. Is that clear?"

"Yes Sergeant Major!"

"Tomorrow you'll be on parade for inspection by his Royal Majesty the King of England and you'll be the smartest looking Company in this man's army!"

On 26 March, the Regiment assembled on the parade ground ready to receive the Royal family. To acknowledge Canada's commitment to England, King George VI and his wife Lady Elizabeth Bowes-Lyon agreed to visit the Canadian troops at Cove. The King took his time inspecting the formations stopping to speak to several soldiers as he walked. When the King passed Jean-Pierre, he smiled then moved on without stopping. *The King of England just looked at me. The bloody King of England whom I swore allegiance to in Montréal.*

Universal Carriers of the 2nd Canadian Infantry Division taking part in a Bren gun display. 6 June 1941 (Probably Cove or Lewes). *Canada. Dept. of National Defence/Library and Archives Canada/PA-177144.*

King George VI and the Queen at Cove, March 1941. Inspecting Canadian troops. *Cent ans d'histoire d'un Régiment canadien-français Les Fusiliers Mont-Royal 1869-1969.*

Chapter 8
Lewes and Blackwater, England
July 1941–September 1941

In late June, the complete Second Canadian Division relocated to the south of England to replace British troops guarding England's coastal area. The Canadian commanders welcomed the new assignment knowing the change of scenery and routine would address their men's growing boredom and frustration from the constant training. The Fusiliers drew responsibility for the area around Lewes, a beautiful little town nestled in a gap in the South Downs. The flat terrain, just seven miles north of the port of Newhaven, provided a potential drop zone for German paratroopers seeking to support a sea borne assault on the port.

During the first week of July, the Fusiliers moved to Lewes, replacing the 2nd Battalion of the 14th South Lancashires. Once settled in, the Regiment kept the men active with training exercises, route marches, Sunday Church parades, and combat patrols on the South Downs. When the troops were not training or patrolling, they went to the historic town of Lewes for meals, beer, and entertainment. For the first time since their arrival in England, the Fusiliers lived in direct contact with the English population, with some soldiers lodging within the town proper. Jean-Pierre loved the water and managed some trips to the coast where he swam in the sea. *There are just 21 miles between Dover and the Germans in Calais,* he thought. *Either they're coming here or we're going there. It can't be long now before we see some action.*

At the end of July, the Regiment received relocation orders. Early in August, a convoy of trucks arrived. Grumbling about having to leave such an ideal posting, the Fusiliers packed their gear, climbed aboard the trucks, and left. The likeable French-Canadians made many good friends in the little town of Lewes and the townspeople were sorry to see the sociable group of soldiers leave.

The trucks carried the Regiment to Blackwater, north of Cove. The region's sprawling fields, forested areas, rivers, and small lakes provided quite a change from Lewes' coastal terrain. Training intensified but the tiny town offered little in the way of relaxation for the men. After two months of isolation and training, the fatigued soldiers felt relieved when notified to prepare for another move.

Canadian soldiers near Lewes, England. *Courtesy of*
http://www.laughingfishonline.co.uk/laughingfish_pub_history.html

Chapter 9
Northease, England
September 1941–February 1942

At the end of September 1941, Les Fusiliers moved to barracks near Northease, a short distance from the tiny village of Southease, on the South Downs. The camp included a good-sized dance hall at Northease Manor with a bar and a bandstand. More importantly for Les Fusiliers, a short drive down a narrow country road or one train stop took them back to Lewes.

From 29 September to 3 October, Jean-Pierre and his regiment participated in exercise Bumper. The countrywide anti-invasion exercise involved 250,000 men and lasted seven days and seven nights. Jean-Pierre and his platoon performed well and the pleasant weather made the experience less gruelling. Officers noted their men's performance and added it to the data they used to track the men's progress since enlistment. Jean-Pierre's chances for promotion were good. A few evenings after Bumper, an excited Maurice sought out Jean-Pierre.

"Today I was asked if I wanted to train with some British Commandos."

"You're kidding?"

"And after they finish training me, I'll help train the Regiment."

"So what did you say?"

"I said yes of course. I'm leaving tomorrow and I'll be gone for about three months."

Jean-Pierre knew Maurice could not turn down such an opportunity. He excelled at everything the army threw at him and he was a natural leader.

"Look after yourself," said Jean-Pierre as he embraced his friend with genuine affection.

Jean-Pierre's relationship with Kathy Lyon became a casualty of his long periods of training with no leave. Her last letter to him explained she met another soldier, a close school friend from her neighbourhood who returned from North Africa. Her rejection hurt his pride, but the pain soon disappeared, lost in his daily duties.

The arrival of another damp and cold autumn signalled the completion of one year of training in England for the men of the Second Canadian Division. Increased incidents of drunkenness, unruly behaviour, and court martials indicated the growing restlessness and frustration in the men. They wanted to see action and help defeat the Germans but the opportunities were few. Even though England no longer feared an imminent invasion, the Germans were still on the offensive elsewhere. Hitler continued his assault on the Soviet Union with Leningrad under siege and Moscow under attack. The Premier of the Soviet Union, Joseph Stalin, pressed England to invade Europe in order to force Hitler to divert troops from the Eastern front. Churchill knew there were insufficient trained troops and equipment available in Britain and Commonwealth countries to support such an endeavour. Though Britain received war material from the United States, Churchill had been unable to convince President Roosevelt to fight against Germany. Consequently, Churchill ordered Commando raids across the Channel to harass the Germans and appease Stalin.

In December 1941, Jean-Pierre's regiment moved to the port of Newhaven to replace the Cameron Highlanders defending the underground fort. However, Jean-Pierre remained in Northease with Company Headquarters to work on the Regiment's bookkeeping backlog. Due to his natural linguistic capabilities and bookkeeping skills acquired in school, he occasionally helped the Regiment with administrative tasks and English to French translations. On weekends, he attended dances at the Northease Manor to occupy his time. His second Christmas abroad came and went without any significant events, other than Christmas cards he received from his sisters and parents.

At the end of December, Jean-Pierre found Maurice waiting for him at the barracks obviously excited about something.

"Jean-Pierre," he exclaimed throwing his arm around his friend's shoulders. "We landed in Norway and fought the Germans."

"What? When?"

"Just last week. It was incredible. I went with British Commandos. It was rough but we caught the Germans with their pants down as they were celebrating the holidays. All the Norwegians wanted to come back with us to England."

Jean-Pierre listened with amazement. While he was celebrating Christmas, his friend went to war. Maurice could hardly contain his excitement.

"We landed at dawn on Vågsøy Island two days after Christmas. The raid involved 570 soldiers, mostly British Commandos with a few Canadians and Norwegians. We attacked German positions and fought some house-to-house battles."

"Any casualties?"

"Yeah, 17 killed including two Canadians and 53 wounded."

The two friends chatted late in to the evening with Jean-Pierre quizzing Maurice about the raid. Later when Maurice returned to Newhaven, Jean-Pierre lay awake in his bunk trying to imagine what it must have been like in Norway.

The next night he wandered over to the dance hall. He entered, lit a cigarette, and walked towards the bar. Soldiers and young women occupied the hall, dancing, sitting at tables with their drinks, or standing in small groups talking and smoking. He surveyed the room and waved to a few of the girls he knew. Then his eyes focused on a couple on the dance floor, more specifically on a beautiful young girl with light brown hair, a radiant smile, and wearing a kilt. He could not remember seeing her at any of the previous dances. The music ended, she joined another young attractive girl, and the two walked arm-in-arm off the dance floor. He continued watching the two girls as they strolled about. When the band started playing again, two soldiers approached them for a dance. Jean-Pierre moved from the bar to get a better view of the young kilted girl. The couple danced as one, her feet easily moving with her partner's through the Quick Step. Jean-Pierre's eyes followed her every move. He could not stop staring at her. As the girl danced, her eyes met his for a brief instant. He quivered as the excitement of the moment traced through his body. The next time she passed, he stared long and hard at her. The young girl stared back and Jean-Pierre felt the blood rush to his face. The music stopped. The girl left her partner and joined her friend pulling her aside and motioning with her head towards Jean-Pierre. The second girl looked in his direction, smiled, and then turned her attention back to her girlfriend. Jean-Pierre put down his beer and made his way through the crowd towards the kilted girl. His mind raced with thoughts of how to introduce himself and what he would do if she refused his invitation to dance. The doubt in his mind slowed his pace and he bumped into another girl who crossed his path.

"Would you like to dance?" he offered, distracted by the collision and looking for some way to excuse himself.

"Luv to," the girl responded.

As they danced, Jean-Pierre silently cursed his momentary loss of confidence. *What the hell was I thinking? The army has trained me to kill and I'm afraid a girl might say no to me.*

Jean-Pierre's preoccupation with his missed opportunity resulted in a very stilted and awkward dance for his partner. Once the song finished, she thanked him and left him standing in the middle of the dance floor. He scanned the hall and noticed the kilted girl alone near the exit. She held an unlit cigarette between her lips as she fumbled through her purse. When he reached her, Jean-Pierre extended his hand placing the flame from his lighter under her cigarette. Startled, she looked up but said nothing.

"What's your name?" asked Jean-Pierre gazing into her blue eyes.

Flustered, she took the cigarette from her lips. "Mary." Her faced blushed. "Mary Baker. What's yours?"

"Jean-Pierre," he said snapping down the cover of the lighter. "Would you like to dance?"

Northease Manor, Northease, England. *Private Collection.*

Mary Baker, England. *Private Collection.*

Chapter 10
Newhaven, England
March 1942–April 1942

In early March, Jean-Pierre rejoined his regiment in Newhaven. He could hardly wait to tell Maurice about Mary.

"I've never heard you go on so much about any girl, not even Kathy," remarked Maurice. By the expression on Jean-Pierre's face and the way he spoke of her, Maurice knew Mary was different. "Now you have someone to come back to," he teased.

Things progressed rapidly for Jean-Pierre and Mary. He learned that Mary was in the Land Army stationed at a farm in Southease. He met her sister Kathleen, her older brothers Peter and Leslie, and heard stories about her younger brother Michael who was in the RAF. Whenever Jean-Pierre received weekend passes, he visited Mary at her mother's boarding house in Brighton.

With the threat of the German invasion now passed and the United States officially in the war against Germany, the politicians, military commanders, and troops wanted to take the fight to the Germans. Pushed by Churchill, military planners looked at several options to put troops ashore in Europe.

Training exercises reached a feverish pitch. Every morning before breakfast, Jean-Pierre and his Company marched six miles from Newhaven to Brighton and then ran the six miles back. More running and other conditioning exercises followed breakfast. They scaled 10-foot high walls without the benefit of ropes and crawled through mud under barbed wire with machine gun bursts of live ammunition fired just over their heads. To add a further sense of realism, the instructors hung severed limbs and innards from animals on the barbed wire to simulate battlefield casualties. They learned how to get through barbed wire by blowing gaps in it or by throwing their body on top as a bridge. They practiced boat landings and scaling the chalk cliffs of the Seven Sisters at Birling Gap. They performed house-to-house fighting in mock-ups of buildings where enemy soldiers and explosive booby traps awaited the careless. Unannounced night exercises roused the soldiers from their sleep, but within a few minutes, they stood outside fully dressed and in formation with their platoon.

On 24 March 1942, the Second Canadian Division took part in an anti-invasion exercise called Hill. It simulated a battle between the Canadian coastal defenders and a large invading German force portrayed by British soldiers, which included surprise boat landings along the English coast.

On 30 March, Jean-Pierre received a Good Conduct Badge and the following week a promotion to Lance Corporal. He celebrated with Maurice over a couple of beer as they reminisced about their experiences in exercise Hill. Maurice looked around then edged closer to Jean-Pierre.

"Before Hill, I was training with our Lieutenant Colonel Menard. We were in a trench getting ready to throw live hand grenades at a dummy machine gun position. Menard takes a grenade, pulls the safety pin, and then drops the grenade."

"Shit! What happened?" asked Jean-Pierre.

"What do you think happened? I wasn't about to throw myself on the grenade. I jumped out of the trench and so did Menard. It went off and fortunately only showered us with dirt."

"Then what?"

"Menard just looked at me kind of menacingly and said 'Shut up about this'". Maurice laughed. "Now I've told you, so don't spread it around because Menard will know it came from me and my career in the army will be done."

On his free weekends, Jean-Pierre went to Brighton while Maurice frequented the nearby pubs, now easily conversing in English. One Saturday evening, Maurice met Old Tom, a weathered poacher who looked older than his 70-years. They talked late into the night exchanging their hunting experiences over several pints of beer. Intrigued with the art of poaching, the next day Maurice accompanied Old Tom to a nearby private estate. Maurice carried a burlap sack that Old Tom had given him. Once on the outskirts of the private estate, they crept their way silently through the woods to an open area.

"See 'ere," said Tom pointing with a bony finger to a number of holes in the ground. "That's where we'll find some rabbit." Raisin sized droppings littered the cropped grass around the holes. "Open that there sack will ya."

Old Tom removed several mesh nets from the sack. Each had a long drawstring around the exterior attached to a wooden peg. He spread the net over the hole completely covering it. He firmly secured the peg in the ground and motioned for Maurice to cover the other holes in a similar manner. Once completed, Old Tom pulled on a pair of worn leather gloves then reached into his jacket pocket for a wooden box.

"There's my gal," he said pulling out a black and white ferret. He stroked her fur gently, removed the net from one of the holes, and put the eager ferret down. It disappeared into the hole and Old Tom quickly put the net back in place.

"It won't be long now," he said with a wide-toothed grin.

Within a few minutes, a rabbit dashed from one of the holes. The net's drawstring tightened enclosing the net around the struggling rabbit. Old Tom grabbed the rabbit with his gloved hands, held it by the neck and back legs then tugged, snapping the rabbit's neck. The ferret succeeded in flushing out two more rabbits. Once satisfied the warren was empty, he placed some chicken livers near one of the holes. The ferret popped its head out of the hole and devoured its treat.

"Another successful hunt, my gal," said Old Tom softly praising the ferret as he gently placed her back in the box.

The rabbit experience left Maurice eager to do his own hunting. Rather than ferrets and nets, he chose a method more suited to his current skills. He borrowed a .22 bore Lee-Enfield rifle from the armoury and headed out to the nearby Peacehaven Golf Club, a local seaside nine-hole course. Closed to members and the public since the start of the war, the course provided the perfect haven for wild animals. In the low rough adjacent to the fairway on the par 5 third hole, he located a rabbit warren with indications of recent activity. He positioned himself behind a grassy knoll and waited. Eventually a rabbit exited one of the holes then hopped towards a gorse bush. It paused and Maurice fired. The sound of the shot echoed over the hills. The rabbit fell to the ground and jerked its legs sporadically before laying still. He quickly stuffed it in a sack and headed back to his barracks before any local troops investigated the noise. As he walked through the trees, he admired the spectacular view of sea. In the distance, he could make out the faint coastline of France. *I wonder what the Germans are doing right now. Are they waiting for us?* Though he had seen battle in Norway, the enemy was caught unawares much like the rabbit. He suspected the next time he encountered them the situation would be quite different.

"Maurice, when do you think we'll see action?" asked Jean-Pierre during supper.

"Sooner than you think," said Maurice quietly.

"What do you know that we don't?"

Maurice checked to see who might be listening in on their conversation. "I'm not supposed to say anything. You remember the commando training that I went on before Norway. Well, they want me to help with some assault and landing training for our regiment. I'll be going to the Isle of Wight at the end of April. You'll be coming some time later. Once we're done with the training, we're going to be sent somewhere."

"It has to be France," stated Jean-Pierre. "And it'll probably be somewhere opposite Dover because that's the shortest distance across the channel."

"Don't you think the Germans know that too? They'll be ready and waiting for us. I think that it'll be the least likely place."

The men continued their debate on the way back to their barracks. That night Jean-Pierre wondered if German soldiers across the channel were having the same type of discussion.

Seven Sisters at Birling Gap, near Seaford, England. *Private Collection.*

Infantrymen of Les Fusiliers Mont-Royal taking part in an assault landing training exercise, England, 26 February 1942. *Cpl. O.C. Hutton / Canada. Dept. of National Defence / Library and Archives Canada / PA-189486/Item no. (creator) 627, fr. 30*

Infantrymen of Les Fusiliers Mont-Royal taking part in an assault landing exercise, England, 26 February 1942. (Seaford). *Cpl. O.C. Hutton / Canada. Dept. of National Defence / Library and Archives Canada / PA-177145/Item no. (creator) 627 fr. 20.*

Canadian infantrymen taking part in an assault landing training exercise, Seaford, England. *Lieut. C.E. Nye / Canada. Dept. of National Defence / Library and Archives Canada / PA-144598/Item no. (creator) 732-6/ Other accession no. 1967-052 NPC.*

Infantrymen of the Canadian Infantry Division scaling a cliff during an assault landing course, Seaford, England. Capt. Frank Royal / Canada. Dept. of National Defence / Library and Archives Canada / PA-213630 /Item no. (creator) 820, fr.20

Chapter 11
Isle of Wight, England
May 1942–July 1942

On 30 April, Maurice and a small group of soldiers left Newhaven for amphibious assault training on the Isle of Wight. The diamond-shaped island, 70 miles west of Newhaven in the English Channel, offered the seclusion needed for the many landing craft and soldiers involved in the training. The advance party took over the facilities of a local nudist resort called Woodside near the town of Ryde. The day after his arrival, Maurice sat with some British troops enjoying his breakfast of bacon and eggs.

"For breakfast, all we get is porridge, bread, and cheese," remarked Maurice to a British soldier sitting opposite him.

"Blimey mate. This is what we get all the time and I suspect it's coming from Canada," said the English commando chuckling at the irony in the situation.

On 19 May, Jean-Pierre and over 500 Fusiliers packed their gear and boarded trucks to take them to Portsmouth on the coast, opposite the Isle of Wight. As Jean-Pierre's truck drove through Brighton, he wondered if Mary was home with her mother or back at the farm. The lengthy convoy travelled along the winding coastal road, passing through towns and villages along the way. The trucks entered the town of Portsmouth and made their way to the docks, already crowded with thousands of soldiers, Bren Gun Carriers, jeeps, and trucks waiting for transportation across the narrow stretch of sea. From the port, ferries carried the Fusiliers to Ryde. *Once we're done here, we have to be going to France,* thought Jean-Pierre as he marched to Whitefield Wood, some five miles from Ryde. They set up their tents in the open fields. Maurice and the advance party joined them later in the day.

Map of Isle of Wight, England. *Private Collection.*

"Jean-Pierre, you wouldn't believe what happened two weeks ago," said Maurice excitedly jabbing his friend's shoulder.

"You're always involved in some sort of adventure," replied Jean-Pierre. He continued storing his gear smiling at Maurice. "Go ahead. What is it this time?"

"I was standing on the observation platform on top of one of the buildings when the air raid siren sounded. Then I saw the bombers. They were Heinkel one-elevens."

"How could you tell?" said Jean-Pierre now engrossed in the story.

"They came so bloody close I could see the black cross on the green fuselage, the swastika on the tail, and the Hun in the cockpit."

"Shit! Where were they going?"

"I thought they were going to attack us but they attacked Cowes instead. There were over 100 bombers and not one British fighter came to the port's rescue."

"Why not?"

"I guess the RAF got caught with their pants down. We were told not to shoot at the planes but they were so bloody low."

"Why couldn't you shoot?"

"They were afraid our spent bullets would fall and injure or kill civilians."

"So what happened at Cowes?"

"The town got hit but it could have been worse. There was a Polish destroyer just sitting there undergoing an emergency refit. She fired at the damn bombers forcing them to attack from a higher altitude. Then she laid a smokescreen. She basically saved Cowes all on her own."

The training on the Isle of Wight was in preparation for a landing in France. As a concession to Stalin and in response to growing pressure from Roosevelt for a second front, Churchill approved Operation Rutter. The division-sized raid on Dieppe scheduled for 22 June would demonstrate the feasibility of securing a port in German occupied France. Approximately 5,000 Canadian troops on the Isle of Wight formed the assault force for the raid on Dieppe. For security purposes, the military quarantined the island, preventing anyone from leaving or arriving. They evacuated all locals except those employed in the island's businesses.

Training started immediately. Every morning, Jean-Pierre carried his full pack over obstacle courses, through tunnels filled with gas, and across rough terrain with machine guns firing live ammunition above his head. He repeated the obstacle course four times each morning. By the end of the day, he had also navigated his way through live minefields and fought in hand-to-hand combat exercises.

Boats transported the soldiers to the Needles, a row of distinctive 300 foot-high columns of chalk rising out of the sea off the western edge of the island. After jumping out of their boats-onto the chalk outcrop, the men attempted to scale the cliffs. Maurice, well prepared from his advanced training, always reached the top first throwing down a rope to help the others climb up the cliff face.

The next phase of the training concentrated on assault techniques, landing, and re-embarking from beaches under live fire. Jean-Pierre practiced coming ashore in either large flat-bottomed landing craft or high speed armed motor boats, called "R" boats.

When Jean-Pierre's "R" boat, carrying 22 other soldiers, approached the beach, he heard a muffled explosion. A wall of water rose up beside the boat drenching its occupants. In between the explosions, he could hear the chatter of machine guns and the sharp crack of bullets passing over their heads. The coxswain throttled back the motors and stopped the boat in the shallows. Jean-Pierre and the other Fusiliers vaulted over the side in waist-deep water and waded towards the shore. Shells exploded ahead of them and bullets kicked up the surf and sand as they ran to their objective. Though this was only training, Jean-Pierre could feel his heart racing. He sprinted across the beach and found shelter behind some large rocks.

"What the hell are they trying to do? Kill us?" yelled a Fusilier also taking cover behind the rocks.

Jean-Pierre suspected he had the same startled, wide-eyed expression on his face.

"I only hope the Germans are as bad shots as our friends are," he replied.

The Fusiliers repeated the practice assaults several times a day. Their only respite came during debriefings of their performance. Jean-Pierre, soaked to the skin and with only corned beef sandwiches as nourishment, was thankful when sundown brought him much-needed rest.

The Fusiliers' six weeks of assault training on the Isle of Wight ended in early June. After much deliberation, the military planners selected the English coast at Bridport for a full-scale dress rehearsal before Operation Rutter. About 100 miles south of the Isle of Wight, Bridport's beach, harbour, and cliffs bore an uncanny resemblance to the Dieppe landscape.

On 11 June at Bridport, exercise Yukon simulated a coordinated landing of 5,000 soldiers. Despite their extensive training on the Isle of Wight, the transportation of troops to the beach lacked the precision needed for the raid. Large flat-bottomed landing craft carrying troops and tanks collided with one another during their approach. Some deposited troops at the wrong beaches or were late arriving. Others beached stern first resulting in soldiers exiting by the boat's seaward facing ramp and into deeper water than expected. These delays upset the exercise's tight schedule leaving the operation in disarray.

"If we had been landing on a beach defended by Germans, we would have been slaughtered," said an officer surveying the fiasco.

After their debriefing from Yukon, Arthur and his platoon relaxed on Bridport's pebbled beach smoking cigarettes. They welcomed the warmth of the sun's rays on their soaked battledress. Some men had stripped down to their shorts and others had open blouses. A portly, elderly man walked by with a cigar in his mouth and his head down. Deep in thought, the man never looked up or acknowledged the troops as he passed them.

"Isn't that Winston Churchill?" asked Arthur to his mates.

"Who?" replied a soldier more interested in emptying the water out of his boots than looking at someone walking along the beach.

"Bloody hell!" yelled their sergeant major. "Put your clothes back on and look like soldiers. That's the bloody Prime Minister of England that just walked by."

Upon reviewing the results of Yukon, British General Montgomery, the commander in charge of all military affairs associated with Operation Rutter, expressed doubts about the feasibility of the operation. The troops returned to their base camps. Jean-Pierre, back at Newhaven, took seven days leave and went to Brighton.

Despite Montgomery's bleak prognosis, senior officers insisted additional training would address Yukon's shortcomings and plans for the attack on Dieppe should proceed. Minus Jean-Pierre and other soldiers on leave, the Dieppe assault force returned to Bridport for exercise Yukon II on 23 June. Marginally better results convinced senior officers to proceed with Operation Rutter, the attack on Dieppe now scheduled for 4 July.

On 27 June, the Second Canadian Division assembled 300 officers for the briefing on Operation Rutter.

"In addition to what you have already heard, there have been a few changes since our last meeting," stated the briefing officer.

A low mumble ran through the assembly. The officers knew from experience that changes were never in their favour.

"The pre-raid bombing of Dieppe has been removed for fear it will cause too many civilian casualties."

"Not if they put the munitions on the bloody targets," whispered an officer to his neighbour.

"In the place of the planned 150 high-level bombers and 4 squadrons of low-level bombers, squadrons of fighter aircraft will rake the beach area with 20 mm cannon fire just before we go ashore."

"Isn't that just fucking wonderful," whispered the officer again.

"The Royal Navy prefers not to have their battleships bottled up in the narrow Channel where they present tempting targets for German U Boats and aircraft. Instead they'll provide destroyers and gunboats to support the landing."

"Those chicken-livered Royal Navy bastards. Jesus Christ. They're sending us on a one-way trip," exclaimed the officer.

"Yes, are there questions?"

Despite some muted comments throughout the crowd, no one answered.

"Right then. It's a go."

On leave in Brighton, Jean-Pierre contemplated how he would handle the situation he now faced, a situation not covered by any of his training. *How do I tell Mary I love her?* He recalled Maurice's words on the train back from the Lyon family. *You will know when the right girl comes along.* When he first set eyes on Mary, he knew she was the one. *How, when and where am I going to tell her?*

One afternoon after tea, they walked along the promenade hand in hand oblivious to all the soldiers, barbed wire, and anti-aircraft guns on the beach.

"Will they be sending you away soon?" asked Mary.

"Probably. I can't believe this training is just to keep us in shape. The men want to see action and are getting frustrated."

Mary stopped walking and turned to face Jean-Pierre. She stared up at him for a moment. He saw the passion in her eyes and he felt the same. He took her in his arms and kissed her. They walked slowly back to the boarding house, and at the door, he kissed her again, but this time more forcefully. She put her arms around his neck and held him tightly. She stared into his eyes then closed hers slowly. They stood for a moment locked in a tight embrace.

"I love you," whispered Jean-Pierre.

That night, when all the guests retired for the evening, Jean-Pierre tiptoed into Mary's bedroom where he found her waiting for him. Lost in the heat of the moment, their bodies came together.

"What if I get pregnant?"

"Well, we'll get married."

"Only if I get pregnant?" Concerned, Mary peered into his dark brown eyes.

"Of course not." Jean-Pierre stifled a laugh and squeezed her arm reassuringly.

The next morning as the lovers sat at the family's kitchen table, Mary's mother fussed over them. "How did you sleep last night?" She served Jean-Pierre a bowl of steaming porridge. "I heard a lot of noise, planes I suspect, and they kept me awake for some time."

Mary looked down at her bowl, her face slowly turning crimson.

"I didn't hear a thing," responded Jean-Pierre putting the napkin on his lap and picking up his spoon.

Jean-Pierre returned to Newhaven from his leave surprised there had been another exercise while he was away.

"You didn't miss anything," said Maurice consoling Jean-Pierre. "We did exactly the same things as Yukon. But this time the sea was calm so at least the boats had a better chance of getting to the beach."

"We must be going to France soon."

"I don't know. We have another exercise coming up called Klondike."

"Not another bloody exercise?" muttered Jean-Pierre. "When are we going to see some action?"

On 3 July, the Fusiliers left their camp and once again travelled to the Isle of Wight. At 1600 hours, Jean-Pierre boarded the Royal Eagle paddle steamship docked at Ryde. A short while later Lieutenant Colonel Menard addressed the Fusiliers.

"Men, this is what we've been waiting for. Tomorrow we attack the port of Dieppe."

A cheer from the men erupted. Jean-Pierre was ecstatic. This was the opportunity to demonstrate what they could do, to not only their officers of the Second Canadian Division but also to themselves.

In addition to the Royal Eagle, 236 other vessels waited at key ports and harbours along the English coast. Rutter involved approximately 5,000 Canadian soldiers, 500 paratroopers, 1,000 pilots, and 2,000 naval personnel.

Deteriorating weather conditions and high winds in the drop zone threatened the safe landing of paratroopers and gliders with troops and equipment. The raid commanders postponed Rutter until the next favourable tide conditions on 7 July. A small advance force, including Maurice, was just 5 miles from the French coast before receiving orders to turn around.

The ships remained in ports along the English coast with the soldiers on board above and below decks. The July sun beat down on the ships, bringing the below-decks temperature to intolerable levels. Jean-Pierre sweated in the stifling heat and waited anxiously for the sound and feel of vibrations from the ship's engines. *Christ, get this bloody ship on its way so we can get out of this hellhole and fight the bloody Germans.*

After several days at anchor, German reconnaissance aircraft detected the fleet assembled in the waters off Cowes. At dawn on 7 July, German bombers attacked, striking two ships but miraculously the bombs passed through their decks and hulls without exploding. The discovery by the Germans of the assembled fleet coupled with further predictions of unacceptable winds in Dieppe resulted in the cancellation of Operation Rutter. Disheartened, the Fusiliers' officers collected photos, maps and other documents related to the raid. During the debriefing of Rutter, all officers stressed the importance of keeping quiet about the cancelled raid.

Damn, thought Jean-Pierre. *We were so close to going.* Frustrated, he disembarked from the Royal Eagle with his Company and returned to Newhaven.

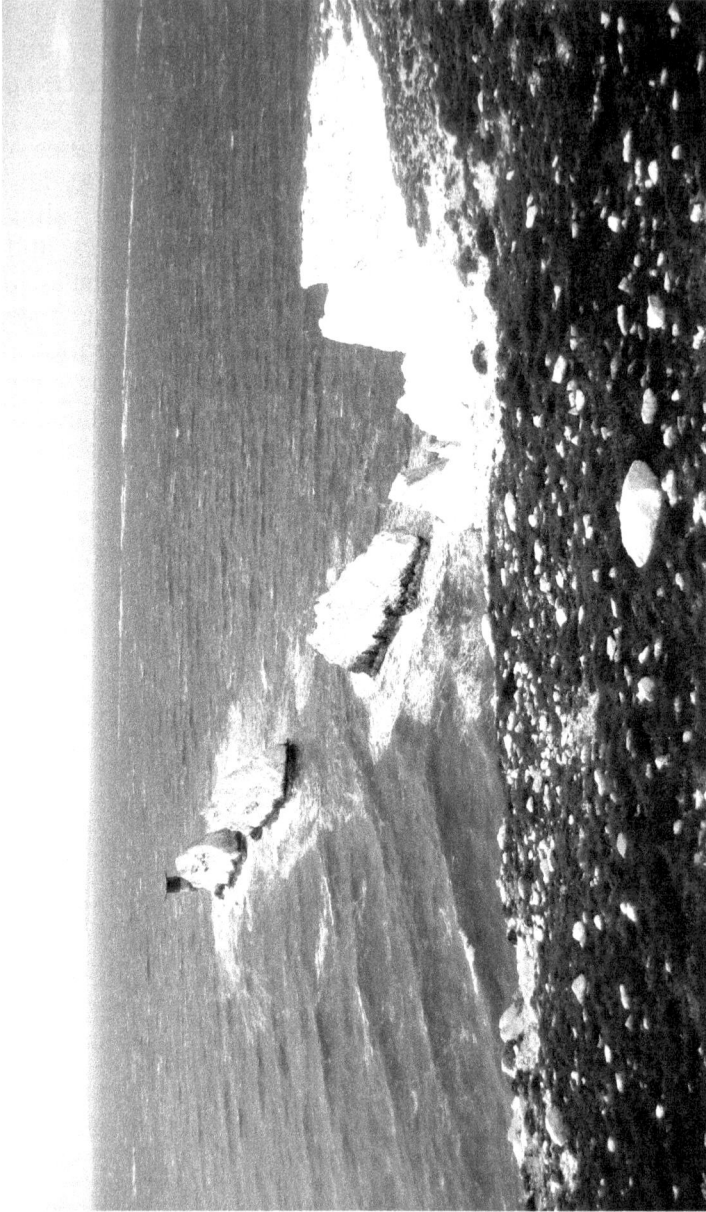

The Needles, Isle of Wight, England. *Private Collection.*

Personnel with a Churchill tank of the Canadian Army which has disembarked from a tank landing craft during Exercise Yukon II. 22-23 June 1942. Isle of Wight, England. *DND / Library and Archives Canada / C-138677/Copy negative C-138677/*

Canadian troops embarking in landing craft during training exercise before raid on Dieppe, France, ca. August 1942. *Canada. Dept. of National Defence / Library and Archives Canada / PA-113244/Item no. (creator) 7252 /Other accession no. 1967-052 NPC.*

Canadian infantrymen disembarking from a landing craft during a training exercise before Operation JUBILEE, the raid on Dieppe, France. England, August 1942. *Canada. Dept. of National Defence / Library and Archives Canada / PA-113243 /*

Chapter 12
Operation Rutter - Aftermath
July 1942

The cancellation of Operation Rutter and the failure to land troops in France weighed heavily on Prime Minister Winston Churchill. General Montgomery, satisfied with the cancellation of the flawed operation, left to take command of the British Eighth Army in North Africa. However, Lord Mountbatten, head of Combined Operations and a rising star in Churchill's eyes, stood his ground. He did not want to let the career enhancing Dieppe raid slip from his grasp. Mountbatten unofficially requested military planners to propose a replacement for Rutter.

The proposal, presented some days later, was audacious in concept. It recommended the raid on Dieppe proceed as originally planned. The next date with suitable tide conditions was 19 August. The planners assumed if the Germans had learned of the raid, they would not believe the British to be foolish enough to attack the same port. The Allied troops did not require further training since they already knew their roles and the details of the raid. To avoid another cancellation caused by high winds in the paratroopers' drop zones, they proposed ship borne commandos instead of paratroopers to take out Dieppe's heavy guns. On 11 July, Mountbatten gave the approval for Operation Jubilee, the resurrection of Operation Rutter.

After the cancellation of Rutter, all units of Les Fusiliers received Privilege Leave. Arthur went to Blackpool with friends to visit the amusement park. The 44-acre Blackpool Park and casino, located 300 miles northeast of Newhaven on the Irish Sea, far exceeded the much smaller Belmont Park he frequented in Montréal. The soldiers enjoyed the distraction the rides and games provided. As they walked along the promenade, they passed a group of British soldiers.

"Hey mates, weren't you in action just recently?"

"Why do you say that?" replied Arthur.

"Your shoulder patch is the Second Canadian Division, isn't it? Didn't you go off to Dieppe or some place in France?"

Arthur remained silent.

"We never went anywhere," blurted Arthur's companion. "They kept us cooped up at the port for bloody days. The Jerries found us and bombed some ships. Then the brass cancelled the damn thing."

Interested in hearing more about the Canadians' experience, the British soldiers invited Arthur and his friends to a nearby pub to continue their discussion.

Jean-Pierre spent his leave in Brighton with Mary. Although discouraged the raid was cancelled, he never spoke of Rutter to Mary or her family. Rested and relaxed he returned to Newhaven on 27 July in high spirits.

Several days later, the Regiment moved to an area just north of Lewes to participate in exercise Grad with the rest of the Second Canadian Division 6th Brigade. The two-day exercise prepared the soldiers who had missed the training on the Isle of Wight. Les Fusiliers Mont-Royal and the South Saskatchewan Regiments formed the attacking units while the Cameron Highlanders were the reserve.

Something must be up, thought Jean-Pierre during the exercise. *The officers look more intense than usual. We can't train forever. We must be going to France soon.*

Chapter 13
Newpound Common, England
August 1942

Immediately after exercise Grad, on 1 August, Les Fusiliers moved again. They arrived in Newpound Common, about 40 miles northwest of Newhaven. The men unloaded their gear from the transport trucks and pitched their tents in some open grassy fields. Maurice's platoon, the Bren Gun Carriers, and the Company Headquarters moved to the town of Horsham about 9 miles from the Fusiliers' tented city. The daily routine of drills and marches paled in comparison to the excitement and commotion associated with Operation Rutter. After being on the verge of engaging the enemy, the return to training in the mud, woods, and streams, dampened the men's fighting spirit. Other than a small pub, there were no women, cinemas, or other activities to distract the soldier's from their dismal living conditions and the monotony of training. Morale dropped to an all time low. In between training, Jean-Pierre continued his clerical duties for "A" Company, thankful to have something else to occupy his mind.

At a meeting in mid-August, the Regimental commanders learned of Operation Jubilee. During the meeting, Canadian senior officers stifled concerns expressed by junior officers regarding the changes made to the support elements of the raid. Orders flowed down to prepare for exercise Ford. The Regiment recalled all officers and enlisted men from leave. Jean-Pierre suspected something important was about to happen. *Where the hell is Maurice? He always knows what's going on.* As soon as Jean-Pierre heard his Company would participate in Ford, he went to the sergeant in charge of the administrative section.

"Sergeant, permission to participate in Ford?"

The sergeant looked at Jean-Pierre sensing his eagerness. "This bloody paperwork will never get done if they keep calling all these damn exercises," he muttered. "All right, go but make sure you're back here when it's done."

"Thank you, Sergeant. I'll be back soon."

Jean-Pierre tidied up his desk then headed to his tent. He spent the evening with members of his platoon preparing equipment, cleaning weapons, and discussing destination possibilities.

"Does anyone know where the Bren Guns are?" asked Jean-Pierre.

"They went off somewhere to the forest around Horsham," replied a member of the platoon.

"Yeah, there wasn't enough room in these wonderful quarters for the limousine jockeys and their beloved carriers. Besides they might have gotten them dirty with all this bloody mud," muttered another sarcastically.

The next morning the few residents of Newpound Common looked on as over 500 khaki-clad soldiers in full kit formed up on the village's grassy fields ready to board their tarpaulin-covered transport trucks.

Personnel of Les Fusiliers Mont-Royal taking part in a training exercise at Newpound Common. 7 August 1942. *Alexander M. Stirton/Canada. Dept. of National Defence/Library and Archives Canada/PA-177146/Item no. (creator) 854 fr. 4*

Chapter 14
Lancing, England
18 August 1942

On Tuesday, 18 August at 1600 hours, Les Fusiliers arrived at Lancing College about 20 miles south of Newpound Common near the coast at Shoreham. The impressive school and its array of buildings, including a huge Gothic style chapel, dominated the landscape. In addition to its many classrooms, the school had boarding houses, theatres, libraries, farmland, and a small-bore rifle range. It was no wonder that, at the outbreak of the war, the British Naval training establishment of HMS King Alfred took over the school facilities.

As he disembarked from the truck, Jean-Pierre could feel the tension and excitement building around him. The men sensed this was the real thing.

"They brought us here in covered trucks. Same as Rutter, remember?" said a Fusilier next to Jean-Pierre. "What the hell do you think that means?"

"Something big is up. This is not an exercise," replied Jean-Pierre matter-of-factly.

The soldiers assembled in one of the College's broad courtyards where Lieutenant Colonel Menard addressed the men.

"Okay boys. This is it. I know I've said this before but tomorrow we land in Dieppe!"

The men shouted their approval. Menard quieted the group and continued his briefing. Once finished, each Company assembled for a review of their assigned tasks and objectives. That evening the troops filed into the school's cafeteria for a hearty meal of mashed potatoes and ham served by the Navy's Ladies Auxiliary.

Arthur devoured his and tried to get a second helping. The server politely refused his request.

"They wouldn't give me seconds but I saw them giving bloody officers seconds and some a third serving," he grumbled when he returned to his seat.

During the meal, the men received paper to once again write their farewells to family members in case they did not return. This sobering instruction changed the soldiers' mood as they sat and composed what might be their final letter. Jean-Pierre looked at the blank paper.

"I'm not writing a letter," he said to the Fusilier sitting next to him. "I have to come back here after the raid. I'm meeting my girlfriend this weekend in Brighton."

Lieutenant Colonel Menard gathered the men in the courtyard, this time for Holy Communion. The Regiment's chaplain, Padre Sabourin, performed the ceremony. Jean-Pierre, a Catholic like the majority of Les Fusiliers, appreciated the opportunity to take Communion and reinforce his spiritual link. Once the service was over, Menard encouraged the troops with a brief pep talk.

With a new sense of urgency, the Fusiliers boarded trucks en-route to the nearby beaches at Shoreham where 26 "R" boats awaited them.

Maurice, in charge of the guard at Horsham, heard about the Fusiliers departure from Newpound Common. Desperate not to miss the exercise, he searched for someone to replace him. Another soldier finally offered to take his place. He quickly collected his gear then managed to secure transportation to the coast at Newhaven. Unable to find his platoon or company, he spoke with an officer explaining the situation. The officer assigned him to Tank Landing Craft # 5, which included Churchill tanks, 30 members from the Fusiliers' "C" Company, and some engineers. Maurice confidently boarded the vessel, at ease going into battle with fellow Fusiliers. He believed his Regiment had the best soldiers in the Canadian army and their extensive training had moulded them into a tightly knit, proud unit ready for battle.

The little armada of "R" boats carrying Jean-Pierre and other members of the Fusiliers headed out to the English Channel to join the large fleet assembling from various points along the coast. In the darkness alone with his thoughts, Jean-Pierre played out the landing etched in his mind from all the briefings. *This is it. We're finally going to France.*

Lancing College, Lancing, England. *Private Collection.*

Chapter 15
Dieppe, France
19 August 1942

Located approximate 80 miles across the Channel from Newhaven and nestled comfortably between two imposing headlands, sat the port and town of Dieppe. Sheer chalk cliffs overlooked the town, harbour, and beach. The broad shingled beach, consisting of large, smooth, pebbles, stretched from the harbour on the west to the cliffs on the east where it narrowed to a sliver of stones. Facing the town, the upward sloping beach stopped abruptly at a low seawall. Beyond the seawall, a wide, open, grassy promenade extended across the town's seafront from the harbour to the cliffs and inward towards the Boulevard de Verdun. The boulevard ran parallel to the beach and separated the promenade from the hotels, shops, tobacco factory, church, and homes. A grand three-storey casino stood at the eastern end of the promenade.

Dieppe's garrison of 1,500 German troops in strategically located fighting positions stood ready to defend the port and other nearby potential landing places along the coast. To improve the Germans' view of the beach and eliminate shelter for any attackers, the Germans were in the process of demolishing the casino. In the interim, they installed MG 42 machine guns that targeted the rocky beach. High fences of coiled barbed wire ran along the beach parallel to the shore, near fortified positions, and along the sea wall. Concrete walls, barbed wire, and booby traps blocked the beach exits. Pillboxes, machine guns, and light anti-aircraft weapons positioned along the promenade and cliffs sat ready and waiting.

Operation Jubilee's plan covered a broad area, including the town of Dieppe. The main attack would take place on Dieppe's beachfront. The plan divided the beach assault in two, Red Beach and White Beach. From roughly the centre of the beachfront, Red Beach ran east as far as the harbour entrance and White Beach extended west to the cliffs just beyond the casino. The plan also called for flank attacks at Blue Beach near the town of Puys and Green Beach near Pourville-sur-Mer. To silence the large coastal guns before the attack, Commandos would land at Yellow I and II Beaches, further east near the towns of Berneval and Belleville-sur-Mer and Orange I and II Beaches westward near the towns of Vasterival and Quiberville.

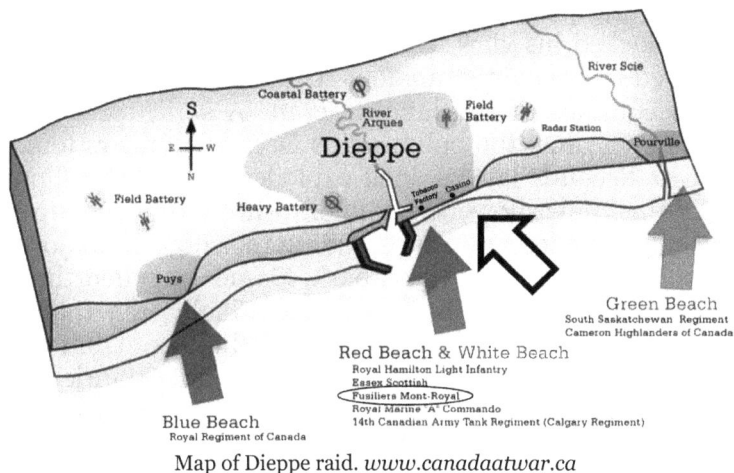

Map of Dieppe raid. *www.canadaatwar.ca*

A warm, moonless night, calm sea, and the steady rumble of the "R" boats' motors lulled Jean-Pierre to sleep. The overnight journey to France left the men with time to think about the approaching battle. Some talked quietly to their neighbours, puffed nervously on cigarettes, prayed, or checked their equipment and weapons. Before dawn, the "R" boats approached the assembly area and the coxswains throttled back their motors. Jean-Pierre woke startled by his boat's deceleration. He fidgeted with his rifle even though he knew his regiment would only land later in the morning. As the reserves, Les Fusiliers Mont-Royal's mission was to provide support on Red or White Beaches to either bolster a unit's attack or exploit a breakthrough of German defences. After the raid, they would conduct a fighting withdrawal to protect soldiers evacuating to the waiting landing crafts.

At 0500 hours the Royal Air Force shattered the silence with their 20 mm cannon fire and bombs. In response, German anti-aircraft fire rose into the blue-violet sky like floating lengths of pearls. Minutes later, British destroyers' guns blasted targets in the town and on the cliffs.

"Holy shit!" exclaimed a Fusilier in Jean-Pierre's boat.

The thunderous noise enveloped the men suppressing any idle chatter. In the distance, large landing crafts approached the beach. Jean-Pierre, his body taut with anticipation, fixed his eyes on the horizon, and waited.

Tank Landing Craft # 5 carrying six Churchill tanks and soldiers, including Maurice, headed towards the beach. The vessel's high steel walls blocked his view. Hidden in the innards of their tanks, drivers revved their engines, anxious to get their vehicles out of the defenceless confines of the landing craft. A series of explosions threw Maurice against the bulkhead as German gunners found the craft's range. Seconds later a shell exploded in the wheelhouse at the rear of the craft, showering soldiers with debris and shrapnel. Another shell exploded amidships, killing the sergeant major and a group of soldiers waiting to disembark. Flames engulfed the stern. Maurice anxiously looked for a way out. Finally, the ramp went down and the first 45-ton Churchill tank lumbered onto shore. Instead of waiting for the remaining tanks to exit, Maurice and 16 other soldiers clambered up the side of the landing craft and jumped into the water. He rushed towards the shore as machine guns fired on the small group. Bullets snapped past his head and streaked through the water beside him, much closer than he had ever experienced in training. From behind came piercing screams and cries of agony, but he kept running. Less than 30 yards in front of their beached landing craft sat a disabled tank, mired in the pebbles. It faced up the sloping beach towards the promenade. *Must be from our boat*. He reached the tank and crouched behind it. *What the hell?* He looked down at his bare feet. He lost his boots somewhere. He could not remember them coming off but they were gone. He shook his head in disbelief and turned to see who else joined him. Three soldiers crouched nearby.

"Where are the others?" he asked.

"We're the only ones who made it," said one of the soldiers wide-eyed and breathing hard.

Dieppe beach, 19 August 1942. Tank Landing Craft #5 in the background. *Library and Archives Canada, DAPDCAP61032, 3192368.*

Maurice looked back towards the water. His landing craft sat at an angle with its ramp down in the water. Smoke and flames billowed from its stern. Bodies of men who left the vessel with him lay mangled in grotesque positions on the pebbles. German machine gunners continued to target the fallen men, their bodies twitching and jumping as bullets struck them. He felt a rage rising. *I have to find a way to get at those bastards.* Bullets zipped past his head as he peered from behind his shelter. He knelt down, looked between the tank's tracks, and saw daylight. He crawled on his stomach dragging his .303 P14 Enfield sniper rifle until he reached the front of the tank. He pulled his weapon forward settling into a prone shooting position. He slowed his breathing and looked through the rifle's scope. Muzzle flashes of German MG 42s sparkled in the dawn light 500 yards away in buildings beyond the promenade. He brought the telescope's cross hair sights to bear on a German soldier standing beside one of the machine guns. He took a deep breath, held it, and slowly squeezed the trigger. The German fell back against the building disappearing from sight. Several other soldiers fell before the Germans discovered his hiding place and concentrated their fire on his position. Bullets ricocheted off the tank's armour and splintered the pebbles, showering him with fragments of stone. A bullet deflected off his helmet. Stunned by the blow, he lay still until the firing on his position ceased. When it did, he began shooting at new targets until the Germans once more directed their deadly stream of bullets at him. This cat and mouse game continued until he ran out of ammunition. He crawled to the back of the tank and cautiously pulled himself out. Hearing the sound of aircraft engines, he looked skyward. A smokescreen descended from a plane flying parallel to the beach, quickly covering everything it passed with billows of thick grey cloud.

After what seemed like an eternity of circling, Jean-Pierre's boat finally slowed. It joined other "R" boats gathering near the craft carrying Lieutenant Colonel Menard.

"We're going to land at Red Beach opposite the tobacco factory," he called to his men using a megaphone. "Our objectives are the buildings across the promenade."

Jean-Pierre visualised the area from photos and mock-ups used in training.

"We're the only French Canadian regiment, boys. Let's show them what we can do. Good luck everyone."

"R" Boats approaching Dieppe, France. 19 August 1942. *Canadian War Museum, 19920085-1113.*

At 0700 hours, the 26 "R" boats sped to shore in three long columns. Jean-Pierre peered over the side. Huge geysers of water rose from the sea, propelled by the explosion of shells as the Germans targeted the approaching boats and landing craft. The low morning sun and a dark haze over the water prevented him from seeing the distant beach. As they drew closer, the sounds of battle intensified and flickering flames appeared through the wispy smoke. His "R" boat suddenly emerged from the smokescreen into bright sunlight. White chalk cliffs faced him. *Jesus Christ! We're nowhere near Red Beach.*

Arthur's "R" boat with #3 platoon, emerged from the protective haze and the German artillery soon found their range. It continued its run to the beach through the murderous onslaught. The "R" boat beside him disappeared into a plume of water and smoke. Once the explosion dissipated, only floating debris marked the spot where 27 young soldiers anxiously waited to land.

"Go. Go. Go. Get the hell out!" yelled the sergeant as the boat stopped 100 yards from the beach.

Arthur threw the 3-inch mortar he carried over the side. He jumped over the hull into waist-deep water holding his rifle above his head with one hand. He bent over and felt for the mortar ignoring the battle raging all around him. He searched for the weapon, his sergeant's words ringing in his ears. *Fraser, when you get to the beach, you had bloody well better have your tube with you or I'll send you straight back for it.* He found the mortar, placed it on his shoulder, and began running through the water towards shore. Despite the weight of the 35-pound mortar, mortar shells in a belted pouch around his waist, his rifle, 200 rounds of ammunition, and hand grenades, Arthur quickly reached the water's edge. A smokescreen from a plane passing overhead hid the promenade and town from his view. Bullets cracked against the pebbles and shells exploded all around. The German gunners continued shooting into the smoky façade, using predetermined settings to sweep the landing areas with deadly fire. Arthur scrambled up the slope joining his mortar team partner. They flopped down in a large depression in the pebbles.

"Where's the base plate?" asked Arthur.

"I threw it over the side but I couldn't find it in the water. I didn't want to stay out in the open too long so I just left it."

"Then there's no bloody point in me carrying this useless thing any further." Annoyed by his partner's miscue, he tossed the mortar tube aside and removed his belt pouch with the three mortar rounds. He turned his attention to the beach. Dead and wounded soldiers lay everywhere. Instead of a greenish-grey colour, the water at the shore now ran red with blood.

Sergeant Major Lucien Dumais, running through the gauntlet of bullets, spotted the two Fusiliers.

"Follow me!" he yelled.

Arthur and his mortar partner rose and ran in a crouch behind the sergeant in the direction of the casino. After several strides, Arthur turned and headed in the opposite direction.

"Where are you going? Dumais said to follow him."

"He'll get us killed. He's too reckless and doesn't give a shit. You know that."

Arthur sprinted down the beach looking for shelter. An officer from the Essex Scottish smoking a cigarette in a cigarette holder strolled towards him, oblivious to the chaos surrounding him. His radio operator walked close behind. *Do they think this is another damn exercise,* thought Arthur.

"I tried to tell them not to let you land because we're losing."

Ignoring the shell-shocked officer's ramblings, Arthur continued along the beach to the wreckage of Tank Landing Craft #5. German artillery and machine guns ignored the craft, content to eliminate the more serious threats elsewhere on the beach. As they approached, an officer called to them.

"I need some volunteers to remove all the explosives in the TLC. There's wounded in there and if a shell were to hit it, they would all be killed."

Arthur boarded the craft. Through the billowing smoke, he slowly moved to the rear. At the stern, he found his way blocked by the wheelhouse door. He forced the door open, peered in, then stopped in his tracks. He slowly backed away, turned, and quickly headed to the bow trying to erase the gruesome images from his mind. He passed a wounded soldier calling out for water. He stopped, looked around, and reached under a blanket covering a dead Fusilier to find his canteen. He spent the rest of the morning removing explosives, never once mentioning the ghastly scene behind the wheelhouse door.

The bow of Jean-Pierre's boat struck bottom, launching his body forcefully into the man seated ahead of him. The German defenders on the cliffs turned their guns and mortars on the new targets. Shells exploded around his boat sending huge columns of seawater skyward amongst the small fleet. He heard the coxswain's urgent call for the men to get out and he jumped over the side. The cold, chest-high water was deeper than he expected. He knew he needed to get out of the water and away from the gunfire. He had to find shelter quickly if he wanted to survive. He shut out the sounds of explosions and focused on the cliffs ahead of him. He pushed himself forward, ignoring bodies floating in the water ahead of him. He reached the shallows, his heart racing on adrenalin as he churned through the water. On the beach, he tried to run faster, but his heavy, water-laden boots slid between the smooth round stones, slowing him down. He reached the cliffs and fell to his knees, exhausted.

He caught his breath, looked around, and saw other Fusiliers hunkered down against the cliff face. He stared at the trail of bodies leading from the boats to the cliffs, his comrades who did not make it through the deadly gauntlet of bullets and exploding mortar shells. He had never seen a dead body before and now they were on grisly display, one only a few yards from where he crouched.

Looking towards the port, he confirmed his boat landed to the extreme right of their intended target of Red Beach to support the Essex Scottish. The morning sunlight illuminated the horrific scene where the Essex Scottish and other elements of the main assault landed. Destruction, devastation, and death covered the beach. The noise was deafening. The furious hail of bullets, mortar and artillery shells rained down everywhere. Explosions threw stones, debris, and dismembered body parts into the air. Immobilised tanks and other vehicles littered the beach. Orange tongues of flames engulfed vehicles struck by the accurate shelling of German guns. Smoke from burning landing craft and vehicles drifted over the battlefield and mingled with the thinning smokescreen laid earlier by British planes. The acrid smell of burnt gunpowder hung in Jean-Pierre's nostrils. *Where are those bastards?* He surveyed the grim scene. *Where the hell are they hiding?*

A nearby explosion startled him. He pressed his body into the rock wall, taking shelter in a deep chalk fissure. Neither the Germans on the cliffs above nor the Canadians at the base of the cliffs could see their enemy, although the Germans held the upper hand. From the cliff tops, the Germans tossed their grenades over the grassy edge. Some grenades tumbled and bounced off the cliff face, exploding harmlessly in the air before reaching the ground. Many landed on the pebbled beach showering the soldiers with a deadly mix of shrapnel and shattered stones.

Jean-Pierre looked for a way to escape the grenade blasts but could see none. *If I stay here, I'll surely die. If I go back to the water or head to the tobacco factory, I'll be a sitting duck.* Despite his rigorous training, nothing prepared him for such a hopeless situation under deadly conditions. The frustration and fear he felt left a dry, bitter taste in his mouth.

As he cautiously rose preparing to join a group of soldiers further along the cliff face, an explosion threw him against the cliff wall and knocked him down. He staggered to his feet and felt an excruciating pain. He gently explored his head with the fingers of his right hand. The top part of his ear moved freely, no longer attached to his head. Warm blood from the wound seeped between his fingers. He looked down to see blood oozing from his left hand. As the energy drained from his body, he collapsed. Lying on his back, he looked up at the pale blue sky with wispy white clouds floating out to sea. The terrible images and sounds of battle disappeared as he drifted into unconsciousness. *I must be dying. It's not so bad.*

German machine gun position. Dieppe, France. August 1942. *Deutsches Bundesarchiv (German Federal Archive), Bild 101I-291-1213-34, Müller, Karl.*

Casino at Dieppe beach 19 August 1942. *Canadian War Museum, 19920085-1112.*

Dieppe beach, France. 19 August 1942. *Canadian War Museum, 19830644-001, Photo Archives T 1.3, Image # 5.*

Dieppe beach, France. 19 August 1942 - wrecked equipment. *Canadian War Museum, 19910238-122, Photo Archives T 5.5, Image # 21.*

Chapter 16
Dieppe, France
Aftermath
19 August 1942

The Royal Navy's plan to evacuate the large number of troops from the beaches failed. Throughout the raid, the German's large coastal guns overlooking the seas at Petit Berneval and artillery closer to Dieppe threatened all vessels close to shore. When the Allies received the signal to withdraw from Dieppe, the deadly gauntlet of bullets from German sharpshooters, machine guns, and mortars targeted the retreating Canadians. Many died running across the open expanse of beach or swimming in the water. They were easy marks for German snipers. The lucky few who managed to board waiting boats were still in danger. Accurate cannon fire from the German's 75 mm beach defence guns sank several Allied craft before they could retreat with their load of dazed survivors.

Arthur watched the British destroyer Calpe come in close to shore passing in front of Red Beach. The German guns bombarded the ship but she continued undaunted and untouched. The Calpe fired a final salvo from her 4-inch guns before turning to the open waters joining the rest of the flotilla heading back to England. *The damn flag is at half-mast. They're leaving us here!*

With the ships gone and the air battle gradually receding, enemy gunfire slackened and a tense calm descended over the battlefield. A Canadian officer, sheltered behind a deserted

Churchill tank, realised further resistance would only result in more casualties.

"I need a volunteer over here!"

A young private lying behind a burned out scout car jumped to his feet. He scrambled to the tank as bullets splintered the pebbles behind him. The officer tied a white scarf to the private's rifle.

"Raise your rifle so they can see the flag then climb up on the tank."

"Yes sir."

The young man raised his rifle and clambered to the top of the armoured vehicle. A single shot rang out. He fell in a heap, blood pouring from a bullet wound to his head. Two men rushed to the soldier's aid. The officer gestured to one of them to take the fallen man's rifle and display it from up on the tank. The soldier cautiously climbed up behind the turret with his arm extended. A bullet knocked him down.

"Bloody hell," cursed the officer. "Bring me one of those prisoners," he shouted to a Canadian guarding captured German soldiers sitting behind the shelter of the tank.

The Canadian soldier motioned with his rifle to one of the Germans who looked nervously at his comrades. The soldier cleared the breech of the rifle to make sure no bullets remained then gave the German the gun. The German climbed up on the tank's hull and slowly raised his arm, extending the rifle and its white flag above his head. Silence followed. German soldiers behind the barricades tentatively moved across the promenade towards the sea wall and the beach where the Canadians waited.

Out of ammunition and seeing the white flag, Maurice threw down his rifle in disgust. While hidden under the tank, his view of the battleground was limited to the narrow window under the hull between the tracks and the telescopic sight on his rifle. Now out in the open, he surveyed the devastation. Canadian soldiers stood in groups around immobilised Churchill tanks, deserted scout cars, and beached landing craft where they had taken shelter from the storm of bullets and exploding shells. Debris littered the beach. Helmets, rifles, equipment, and supplies lay where thrown by soldiers or by explosions. No matter where he looked, he could not avoid the sight of the dead. They floated in the water, rocking gently in the surf. Near the seawall, formations of soldiers lay along its length cut down by the unseen machine gun firing enfilade from a bunker at the end of the wall. Twisted, grotesque uniformed shapes identified men torn apart by explosions. The bodies of radio operators, a preferred target of German snipers, dotted the beach with their cumbersome equipment still strapped to their backs.

Jean-Pierre regained consciousness. Sensing movement around him, he raised himself on an elbow, the hard round stones jutting into his body. He moaned as the sudden motion caused a stabbing pain in his head. His surroundings slowly came into focus. German soldiers in grey uniforms, black jackboots, and coalscuttle helmets walked cautiously on the beach with their pistols, rifles, and machine guns at the ready. They gestured with their weapons for the Canadians to raise their hands and moved groups of soldiers away from the cliffs towards the promenade. There were soldiers everywhere but to Jean-Pierre the beach was eerily silent. Drawn by Jean-Pierre's movements and the sight of his bloodied head, a Fusilier knelt beside him. The soldier's mouth moved but Jean-Pierre heard nothing so he pointed to his ears shaking his head. The Fusilier nodded and examined his wounds. He took a white, gauze bandage from his kit, wrapped it around Jean-Pierre's head, and then placed another bandage around his mangled left thumb. Prodded by a German's bayonet, they joined a group of Canadian soldiers walking at gunpoint towards the promenade. Feelings of shame and guilt replaced the pain in Jean-Pierre's head as he walked under the guard of jubilant German soldiers. The thought of failing to contribute towards his regiment's objectives and not firing a single shot from his rifle ate away at him. They reached the grassy promenade where the Germans directed the disorganised mass of prisoners towards the town. Jean-Pierre looked around in disbelief. *There must be thousands of us here. Didn't anyone get away?*

   The Germans marched their assembled prisoners up the narrow cobblestone streets of Dieppe. The debris from hundreds of shattered windows caused by explosions littered the streets. The victorious Germans took great satisfaction in showing their prize of defeated Canadians to the Dieppois. The citizens lined the streets from Rue Sygogne to Avenue Pasteur leaning out their windows to watch the sorry procession of dejected soldiers. The rag tag collection of men in torn, bloodied, or incomplete battledress bore no resemblance to the proud soldiers who landed on the beach hours ago. Many struggled to walk and some required assistance. Jean-Pierre marched with his hands in the air past the curious civilians lining the narrow streets. He felt embarrassed and humiliated. *How could things have gone so wrong? Where were they taking us?*

The prisoners arrived at the Hôtel-Dieu Hospital where the Germans herded them to the open areas surrounding the hospital. Some men, knowing the Germans executed military prisoners in Poland, whispered their fears to others. They looked anxiously about, as if seeking a way to escape their captors. The tension broke when doctors and nurses exited the hospital to treat the wounded. Stretcher bearers took the seriously wounded inside while the rest remained outside on the grass. The number of men requiring treatment overwhelmed the local French doctors. Canadian medical officers and medics who survived the battle joined forces with the French and German medical staff. Every sort of injury possible faced the doctors, from simple scratches requiring basic care to life threatening wounds requiring complex surgical interventions. Arthur watched as a Canadian officer came out of the hospital and rushed over to a nearby German soldier.

"Please, we need help to find some B+ blood for a wounded man."

"I'm sorry but I don't have time to look. German soldier's identification tags carry their blood type. Did the Canadian army think that none of their soldiers in battle would perhaps need blood? I have no time for this foolishness."

The Canadian officer walked between the soldiers resting on the grass desperately asking for their blood type.

After receiving treatment for his wounds, Jean-Pierre sat with his elbows on his knees and his head in his hands deep in thought. He regretted not writing a letter to his parents and Mary. *How will they know where I am? What will Mary think when I don't call or show up this weekend?*

Dieppe beach 19 August 1942 - German soldiers taking stock of wrecked equipment. *Canadian War Museum, 19910238-122, Photo Archives T 5.5, Image # 19.*

Dieppe beach 19 August 1942 - disabled Scout car. *Canadian War Museum, 19910238-122, Photo Archives T 5.5, Image # 30.*

Dieppe 19 August 1942 - prisoners marching through the streets of Dieppe. *Canadian War Museum, 19790170-001, Photo Archives T 5.1, Image # 15.*

Dieppe 19 August 1942 - prisoners marching through the streets of Dieppe. *Canadian War Museum, 19830136-001, Photo Archives T 1.3, Image # 14.*

Canadian POWs marching through the streets of Dieppe, 19 August 1942. *Canadian War Museum, 19910238-122, Photo Archives T 5.5, Image # 15.*

Canadian soldiers of the 2nd Canadian Infantry Division taken prisoner by the Germans in the raid on Dieppe, Operation "Jubilee" 19 August 1942. *Canadian War Museum, 19900076-952, Photo Archives T 1.3.*

Canadian casualties awaiting treatment Dieppe, France , 19 August 1942. *Canadian War Museum, 19910238-122, Photo Archives T 5.5, Image # 18.*

Canadian casualties awaiting treatment Dieppe, France , 19 August 1942. *Canadian War Museum, 19830136-001, Photo Archives T 1.3, Image #18.*

Germany Army personnel documenting Canadians casualties at Dieppe, 19 August 1942.
Canadian War Museum, 19910238-122, Photo Archives T 5.5, Image # 25.

Dieppe prisoners, 19 August 1942. (English translation of German text at bottom of photograph: They landed in Germany. Prisoners. They fought for nothing.) *Canadian War Museum, 19830644-001, Photo Archives T 1.3, Image # 16.*

Chapter 17
Newpound Common, England
20 August 1942

At Newhaven, vehicles transported the wounded to hospital and the other survivors to temporary barracks. From the Fusiliers who had not participated in the raid, the Regiment assigned several officers and the Regiment's new chaplain the unpleasant task of going to Newpound Common to collect the personal effects of all the missing and dead soldiers. Of the 584 Fusiliers who took part in the raid, only 125 returned.

At Newpound Common, it was evident the occupants of the deserted camp intended to return after the so-called exercise Ford. Clothes lay strewn on cots and on the floor. An unfinished game of cards rested on a table with each player's hand face down opposite empty chairs. Newspapers and magazines sat scattered on desks and tables.

"It's like time has stood still since the moment they left," said an officer.

A small, black and white mongrel watched intently from his master's cot as the officers moved through the tents. The gravity and magnitude of the task weighed heavily on their minds. They each carried a list of names of those who had returned, for it was much simpler to compare names against this shorter list. Under the watchful eyes of the mascot, they went from cot to cot, under a shroud of silence and sorrow searching for the occupant's name on the list. If it did not match, they carefully and respectfully removed the missing Fusilier's personal effects.

An officer moved to Jean-Pierre's cot and picked up a photo of a pretty, young girl. He looked at it for a moment and then put it in a box with Jean-Pierre's playing cards, letters, cigarettes, and books. He sealed it and clearly marked D61894 LAEKAS, JEAN-PIERRE on its side before moving on to the next cot.

Chapter 18
Envermeu, France
19-20 August 1942

"Attention! All those who can walk, form a line on the street," yelled a German officer.

Jean-Pierre got up and joined the men assembling, as did Arthur and a bootless Maurice. The lengthy column walked from the Hôtel-Dieu Hospital down Avenue Pasteur and Boulevard du Général de Gaulle towards the port. They crossed two bridges and continued marching on Avenue de la République, Route d'Envermeu, and Rue Jacques Monod leaving the town of Dieppe behind them. The long procession of prisoners continued marching through the French farmlands and small villages along the winding country roads. Jean-Pierre had plenty of time to think about his predicament. *Where are they taking us? What are they going to do with us when we finally stop marching?* Hungry and tired, the prisoners stopped 8 miles later at the town of Envermeu, the site of German Divisional Headquarters of the 302nd Infantry Division that defended Dieppe and inflicted such grievous losses on the attacking Canadians. The Germans separated the men, confining the officers in the town's church and the enlisted men in a large abandoned factory.

The strain of capture compounded by the lengthy march had long since depleted the adrenalin that carried the soldiers through the battle. Exhaustion and doubt replaced their earlier energy and enthusiasm. In the absence of officers, British Regimental Sergeant Major Beesley of No. 3 Commando, took charge and got the thousands of men settled in at the factory. He quickly established himself as the prisoners' leader. He gave them a pep talk on the trials and tribulations of being a prisoner of war, including recommending that all privates claim a higher rank when the Germans register them.

"The Geneva Convention does not permit the Germans to force prisoners who are non-commissioned officers and commissioned officers to work, however privates are fair game. Forewarned is forearmed!"

The Germans supplied the hungry prisoners with black bread and a big cauldron of ersatz coffee. The men had no cups so they took turns drinking the coffee from empty tin cans strewn on the factory floor.

"How are your feet?" asked Jean-Pierre after he located his friend.

Maurice was carefully unwrapping a blood soaked bandage that swathed his left foot.

"They better not be marching us anywhere soon," he muttered. "I should have bloody well taken a pair of boots from the beach."

Arthur wandered around the empty factory to see what he could scrounge. He discovered a door near the back of the building. He looked over his shoulders to make sure there were no guards watching and then slowly opened the door. He poked his head in and saw what looked like a temporary kitchen, presumably where the Germans prepared the coffee and stored the bread. *They must've known we were coming.* A wood staved barrel stood just beyond his reach. Satisfied no one was in the kitchen he went inside and peered into the barrel. It contained stalks of celery. He took several sticks and quickly left the room shutting the door behind him.

"What have you got there?" asked a sergeant catching sight of Arthur trying to conceal something in his blouse.

"Some sticks of celery," responded Arthur in a tone lacking military formality.

"Go back and get me some."

"Pick it yourself," said Arthur abruptly as he walked away.

Confined in the abandoned factory and surrounded by armed German guards, the prisoners spent a restless night sleeping on the cinder floor. Jean-Pierre slept fitfully waking frequently from his throbbing wounds and the nightmares of battle.

POW's marching to Envermeu, France. 20 August 1942. *Canadian War Museum, 19910238-122, Photo Archives T 5.5, Image # 7.*

Prisoners from Les Fusiliers Mont-Royal, 20 August 1942. Envermeu, France. *Courtesy of http://wehrmacht-awards.com/forums/showthread.php?p=4742012.*

Chapter 19
Verneuil-sur-Seine, France
20 August 1942–2 September 1942

The following morning, the Germans herded the POWs to the nearby train station. They lined up in front of wooden boxcars. A French sign written on the side of each boxcar indicated its capacity of 40 men or 8 horses.

"Jesus Christ," muttered a Fusilier to the man queued in front of him. "The damn Huns are on some of the boxcar roofs with machine guns."

The Germans crammed the men into the wagons at gunpoint.

"There must be 80 of us in here," said Jean-Pierre standing shoulder to shoulder with his comrades.

The men chatted nervously. They had no idea where the Germans were taking them. Just over an hour later, the train stopped at Verneuil-Sur-Seine near Paris. The German guards marched the Canadians to an open field outside the perimeter of an abandoned First World War French military camp. The POWs received water in pails but no food. After thoroughly searching the prisoners, the Germans guided them to some dirty deserted barracks within the camp. Broken glass from windows crunched under their boots, bunks lacked bed boards, and empty cans, cigarette butts, and decomposed food littered the floor. The latrines smelled foul due to the lack of running water. The men tried to clean up their quarters as best they could, uncertain how long they were going to stay.

First World War French military camp. Verneuil-sur-Seine, France. *Courtesy of http://aefcollections.forumactif.org/*

The next day interrogations started. When Arthur's turn came, he squared his shoulders, stared straight ahead, and stated his name, rank, and identification number.

"Why didn't you land further away from the beach and our defences? We had nothing there," asked the German officer.

Arthur repeated his name, rank, and identification number.

"We were waiting for you and you were late. You were supposed to come earlier," continued the officer.

Arthur did his best to hide his surprise at the German's remarks but he recalled the words of the British soldier at the Blackpool amusement park after the cancellation of Operation RUTTER. *Your shoulder patch is the Second Canadian Division, isn't it? That's the division that went off to Dieppe or some place in France.*

Back in the filthy barracks, Arthur discussed his interrogation with the other Fusiliers. They all recounted similar questioning.

"Remember the attack by the German planes when we were waiting at the Isle of Wight?" said a Fusilier. "How could Churchill and Mountbatten have been so stupid to send us to Dieppe after that?"

"They knew we wouldn't be able to catch the Germans by surprise, but they sent us anyway, the bastards," said a soldier squatting on the floor next to Arthur.

"The Jerry that interrogated me knew of the conscription crisis in Canada," added another Fusilier. "He even knew the date was last April and Quebec had voted against it while the rest of Canada had voted in favour."

"They probably knew more about this bloody raid than we did," said another prisoner.

After nine days of interrogations, the Germans led the prisoners back to the nearby rail yard. Weak from eating only a watery soup each day, they queued in front of the train. Jean-Pierre boarded an already crowded boxcar. He noticed the straw covered floor and an empty bucket in the corner presumably to collect the men's waste. *This is not going to be a short train ride.*

Typical French boxcar- 40 men or 8 horses, 1940. *Courtesy of http://www.in-honored-glory.info/html/stories/ifanderson.htm*

As Arthur climbed up, he saw Sergeant Major Dumais in the corner of his car speaking with two other soldiers, one of them a Fusilier called Cloutier. Arthur overheard them talking about escape and approached the three men.

"Sergeant Major Dumais. I would like to join you when you go," said Arthur.

Dumais stared at him. Arthur anxiously wondered if he remembered the incident on the beach.

"We'll be jumping from the train. Can you handle that?"

"Yes Sergeant Major."

Dumais nodded and explained his plans to the four men. Once the train began moving, Dumais and Cloutier started working on the wire grating covering a narrow window. They loosened one end and forced the grating until its fasteners broke free from the dry wooden frame. Sergeant Major Dumais squeezed through the small opening followed by Cloutier. Arthur, hands gripping the window frame, prepared to exit.

"Wait. There's not enough room out here until we've jumped," called Cloutier through the opening.

A short while later, the train slowed on a turn and the prisoners heard the chatter of machine guns from the roof, presumably shooting at the two escapees. With the Germans alerted, Arthur decided to wait for another opportunity.

The train travelled for about two hours before stopping in Belgium. The Germans ordered the men to disembark then separated the French speaking Fusiliers Mont-Royal from the rest of the prisoners. Representatives of the German-sponsored Vichy French government addressed the Fusiliers, praising their courage and bravery. To acknowledge their solidarity with the French Canadians and hoping to gain the same in return, they gave each Fusilier canned food, bread, and cake. Their attempt to create dissension failed when the Fusiliers snubbed the Vichy French and shared their food with English-speaking prisoners from other regiments. Disappointed with the Fusiliers' reaction, the Germans ordered the men back into the boxcars.

Jean-Pierre lost track of time and the days ran one into another. The train travelled through the occupied territories of Belgium and Holland and then into the Ruhr valley in Germany. Occasionally it waited on sidings for the tracks ahead to clear of other traffic. While stopped, the Germans sometimes opened the car doors and gave the men another loaf of bread and a little water. During these breaks, the Germans did not permit the prisoners to disembark, but the men took the opportunity to empty their waste buckets. The boxcar's oppressive heat and unbearable stench of sweat, excrement, and vomit was worse than anything Jean-Pierre had ever encountered. Some of his comrades lay crumpled on the stinking soiled straw while others stood unconscious or a sleep, held upright by the tight press of bodies around them. Determined to endure this ordeal, Jean-Pierre blocked the sickening sights and sounds surrounding him with pleasant thoughts of England and his last passionate embrace with Mary.

CANADIAN NATIONAL TELEGRAPHS

Form 6102B

Exclusive Connection with WESTERN UNION TELEGRAPH CO.
Cable Service to all the World
Money Transferred by Telegraph

D. E. GALLOWAY, Assistant Vice-President, Toronto, Ont.

RECEIVER'S NO.   TIME FILED   CHECK

CLASS OF SERVICE DESIRED

FULL-RATE MESSAGE	X
DAY LETTER	
NIGHT MESSAGE	
NIGHT LETTER	

PATRONS SHOULD MARK AN X OPPOSITE THE CLASS OF SERVICE DESIRED; OTHERWISE THE MESSAGE WILL BE TRANSMITTED AS A FULL-RATE TELEGRAM

Send the following message, subject to the terms on back hereof, which are hereby agreed to
Veuillez expédier la dépêche suivante aux conditions mentionnées au verso auxquelles je consens par les présentes

For French translation   OTTAWA AUGUST 24 1942

MR MICHEL LAEKAS
1793 BEAUDRY
MONTREAL PQ

7328 SINCERELY REGRET INFORM YOU D61894 LANCE CORPORAL JEAN PIERRE

LAEKAS OFFICIALLY REPORTED MISSING IN ACTION STOP FURTHER INFORMATION

FOLLOWS WHEN RECEIVED

Officer i/c Records

PREPAID
(W.E.L. Coleman), Lt.-Col.
(Cas.)

Missing in Action telegram sent to Jean-Pierre's father on 24 August 1942 from the Canadian Army. *Private Collection.*

127

Chapter 20
Lamsdorf, Germany - Stalag VIIIB
Prisoners of War
3 September 1942

The train stopped at the Sowin train halt just outside the town of Lamsdorf, Germany, on 3 September 1942. The wooden door slid open and the German soldiers, with their guns at the ready shouted for the men to get out. The five-day train journey from Verneuil-sur-Seine left Jean-Pierre weak. His aching legs prevented him from jumping out so he bent down, sat on the boxcar's ledge, and lowered himself to the ground. He stood leaning against the side of the train, his eyes trying to adjust to the bright sunshine. Other POWs lay on the filthy boxcar floor unable to move or stand. The German guards ordered the able-bodied prisoners to carry the wounded off the train. Jean-Pierre watched as his mates removed four still bodies, soldiers who died of their wounds in transit. Still emotionally drained by what he witnessed on the Dieppe beach, he felt nothing as the corpses of his fallen comrades passed him.

Sergeant Major Beesley called them to assemble bringing Jean-Pierre back to reality. On unsteady legs, he joined the formation of POWs. The Germans led the ragged column of men past the train halt to the end of the road where they turned left and passed a cemetery, its sight sending a nervous murmur through the ranks. Just beyond the cemetery, they turned right onto a narrow road, paved with grey, granite setts and lined with chestnut trees. The column of battered and weary soldiers contrasted starkly to the tranquil country scenery and the majestic trees. They hobbled, staggered, and walked for some distance until the winding road led them to a large clearing.

Jean-Pierre saw a high, multi-strand, barbed wire fence enclosing a vast compound. At regular intervals outside the fence stood wooden guard towers, each fitted with a mounted machine gun and searchlights. The towers rose high above the fence, providing the guards with a commanding view of the camp's interior and the cleared area outside the fence extending to the woods.

"Let's show these Kraut bastards what you Canadians are made of," shouted the Sergeant Major.

As one, the formation squared their shoulders, straightened their backs, and marched towards the camp in step with arms swinging. As he approached the entrance, Jean-Pierre looked up at a nearby tower. The German soldier leaning on the machine gun stared back at him over the gun's barrel. Inside the camp, he marched past rows of barracks behind more barbed wire fences. German soldiers stood close by watching the procession, some with leashed Doberman Pinschers snapping and straining to reach the new prisoners. Though doubt and fear clawed at Jean-Pierre's mind, he performed his best version of a parade ground march into the camp.

Stalag VIIIB, situated in a pine forest near the Czechoslovakian border in German occupied Poland, consisted of eight compounds surrounded by two concentric nine-foot barbed wire fences and guard towers every 100 yards. Several hundred German soldiers provided around-the-clock surveillance of the camp's inmates. Another 100 soldiers with armoured cars stationed at a nearby base provided additional support, should the need for reinforcements arise.

The German guards led the column of Canadians along the camp's network of roads separating the many buildings. As they passed several compounds, British prisoners shouted words of encouragement to the new arrivals. *There must be thousands here,* thought Jean-Pierre as he walked past the prisoners cheering and waving behind the barbed wire.

The Germans directed them to an open area, counting the men as they entered and told the POW in charge to form up the men on the parade ground. Sergeant Major Beesley barked the order and the men quickly got into formation.

"Before you are sent to your compound, you will have your hair cut and then you will be taken to the bathhouse in groups of 20 for delousing. Your clothes will also be deloused," said the German officer. "This is to prevent the spread of typhus from your lice and other vermin that found their way onto your clothing and bodies."

Uneasy whispers ran through the formation, the men remembering the numerous atrocities committed by Germans against Polish civilians and soldiers, including using the pretext of a shower to gas their victims. In response to this unrest, the German guards brought their rifles and machine guns to bear on the assembled troops. Maurice turned and looked with apprehension at Jean-Pierre who stood nearby. Both men realised the futility of any attempt to resist. Resigned to their fate, Maurice and Jean-Pierre followed the long line of men to the barber's station. A barber sheared their heads then they proceeded to the bathhouse. Jean-Pierre removed his clothes and stuffed a piece of paper with his name on it in his blouse pocket. *They're going to a lot of trouble if they just plan to gas us.* Much to his relief, the showers emitted streams of water and not clouds of gas. Jean-Pierre washed away the dirt, grime, and the blood as best he could with one hand, taking care to avoid putting pressure on his swollen thumb and his ear. The sensation of water on his body and the task of washing occupied his mind. As he dried himself and dressed in his deloused clothing, his thoughts returned to Dieppe. *Despite all my training, I failed to make it to the tobacco factory. Unlike Maurice, I never fired my rifle at those damn Germans. I never moved from under the cliffs. By doing nothing, I survived the terrible slaughter, while so many died fighting.* The guilt he felt gnawed away at him.

From the showers, he went for his registration and photograph.

"Name, rank, and serial number," stated a German officer in perfect English.

"Laekas," he responded. "Lance Corporal, D61894."

"How do you spell your name?"

"L A E K A S," he said slowly.

The German officer nodded. He wrote the information on a chalkboard with a cord attached.

"Hang this around your neck then stand in front of the camera."

They're photographing us as if we're criminals. Jean-Pierre felt ashamed. The German took the photo, retrieved the chalkboard, and gave Jean-Pierre a length of string. On it hung a small, flat, rectangular metal identification tag. A line of elongated holes divided the piece of metal into two sections. He fingered the tag. *They probably snap off one piece when someone dies.* On either side of the serration, the tag contained the same information, Stalag VIIIB, 26652. *I'm not prisoner 26652. I can't be.* He looked down at the string around his neck. *I'm still Fusilier D61894 and will always be a Fusilier until this damn war is over.*

Chapter 21
Lamsdorf, Germany - Stalag VIIIB
The Rules
3 September 1942

Stalag VIIIB had a large hospital called the Lazarett, to deal with the POWs' ailments. A German officer ran the hospital, but with the exception of a German Chief Dispenser in control of the stores, the rest of the staff consisted entirely of prisoners. They included general physicians and surgeons, psychiatrists, anaesthesiologists, and radiologists. The hospital, located on six acres of land in the forest, had 11 concrete buildings. Six of these buildings were parallel blocks or wards, each holding from 70 to 100 patients. The hospital had the capacity to serve outpatient needs of 30,000 men.

A German officer sent all the prisoners with wounds to the hospital for an examination by a doctor. They walked under guard for about a mile outside the camp perimeter, some staggering, some leaning on their comrades for support, and some carrying the seriously wounded on stretchers. Jean-Pierre held his left hand close to his waist. Swollen to almost twice its normal size, it itched and throbbed. They finally reached the hospital and queued waiting to be processed.

"Your number and nature of wounds?" asked a bored orderly.

"D61894. My ..."

"Not that number," interrupted the orderly. "I need your stalag number."

Jean-Pierre reached for his identification tag.

"26652," he mumbled, humiliated and annoyed by his new number. "My ear and my hand," he said pointing to his head and extending his swollen hand.

The orderly noted the information on a form and told him to join the line waiting for a doctor's examination. An hour later, Jean-Pierre finally stood in front of a doctor. He removed the bandage from Jean-Pierre's head and examined his ear.

"You're lucky. The wound looks worse than it actually is. A small piece of your ear is gone but it's healing nicely. How is your hearing?"

"When it happened, I couldn't hear but it seems to have come back."

"Let's have a look at your hand." The doctor gently removed the soiled bandage. "It's a bit of a mess. It's infected and the best thing at this point would be to amputate your thumb to save your hand."

"No damn way, sir," said Jean-Pierre as he pulled his hand from the doctor's grip. "Just clean it up and give me a bandage."

The doctor looked at the determined expression on the young soldier's face. With other patients waiting, he did not have time to argue.

"Fine," he said shrugging his shoulders. "I hope for your sake it works out."

He re-opened the semi-sealed wound and cleaned it with disinfectant. Jean-Pierre did not flinch. The doctor told an orderly to bandage his thumb and to clean and bandage his ear.

"I want you to come back here in three days. Then I'll tell you whether or not you're going to keep your thumb," said the doctor putting his hand on Jean-Pierre's shoulder.

When he got back to the camp, Jean-Pierre took stock of his surroundings. Similar to all the other compounds he passed on the way in, a barbed wire fence enclosed the Canadian compound. The fence surrounding their barracks resembled a trapezoid, with one side a bit longer as it went off at an angle following the tree line. Four long grey concrete barracks numbered 19 to 22 sat parallel to one another with a parade ground facing the first barracks near the compound entrance. Each barracks consisted of two sections or huts called "A" and "B" that accommodated 140 men.

Jean-Pierre entered his new home at barracks #19 hut B. The guards had randomly separated the prisoners when they first arrived so Jean-Pierre shared his hut with POWs from various regiments captured at Dieppe. Some were Fusiliers while others came from the Cameron Highlanders of Canada, Royal Hamilton

Light Infantry, Calgary Tanks, Royal Navy, and British No. 3 Commandos.

Rows of triple-tiered wooden bunks filled the hut. Wooden bed-boards supported the bunks' straw mattresses. A single thin wool blanket lay folded on each bed. A small open area contained three tables and six benches as well as a coal-fuelled oven. A large horse-watering trough divided the two sections of the barracks and served as the bathing station for the 280 men. After finding his bunk, Jean-Pierre walked out to the parade ground looking for the latrine. Facing his barracks near the compound's fence, a smaller concrete building housed the single latrine. He walked in and gagged. It was a 40-holer similar to Valcartier's including the foul smell.

On the other side of the camp road, a compound with men in RAF uniforms watched the Canadians intently.

"Hey mate. Where're you from?" yelled a POW standing behind the fence.

"Canadian army, Second Division," replied Jean-Pierre. "We landed at Dieppe but..." Jean-Pierre could not continue.

"Don't worry, mate. The Krauts may have won the battle, but they haven't yet won the war. Not by a long stretch. Don't let it get to you. I've been here since Dunkirk."

The POW's words provided some comfort to a despondent Jean-Pierre. He waved to the man before returning to the barracks. *He seemed pretty healthy and cheerful considering he's been here for two years.*

That evening Jean-Pierre, Maurice, Arthur, and the other Fusiliers listened to a briefing given by Sergeant Major Beesley.

"Gentlemen, I have spoken with our RAF neighbours who gave me an appreciation of what we can expect while we're here. We fought together and now we'll endure this together."

I didn't fight, thought Jean-Pierre.

"I suspect we have a long road ahead of us. The Germans have the upper hand right now, but make no mistake about it, the war will end, and we'll get out of here," he paused and looked at the men before continuing.

"We left many good friends and comrades back in Dieppe, but there is little we can do here to avenge their deaths. To throw our lives away in irrational and individual acts of sabotage or murder will be pointless. You're proud soldiers and I expect you to behave and dress accordingly." He surveyed his attentive audience but the men stood still, waiting for him to continue.

"You will follow the camp's regulations or I personally guarantee I'll make your life even more miserable during your stay here." He looked again at the men with a deliberate and unyielding stare as he emphasized the word will. No one said a word.

"I have good news. Your Lieutenant Colonel Menard, though wounded in the attack, made it back to England safely."

The assembled Fusiliers let out a roar. After the noise died down, Beesley continued.

"I want you to know that we have in our midst a man who chose to join us as captives, rather than return to England on August 19th."

The men looked around wondering who he was talking about.

"His name is Captain John Foote, the Royal Hamilton Light Infantry's chaplain. I've been told not only did he help numerous wounded soldiers back to the waiting boats, but he also returned voluntarily to the beach so he could help those of us captured. Just in case any of you are feeling sorry for yourselves, think of the sacrifice the padre has made."

Many men nodded their heads, having witnessed his selfless and courageous acts on the beach.

"Now to the details," he said looking at several sheets of paper. "Your day will begin at 0600 hours when, regardless of the season, weather, or temperature, the compound's loudspeaker system will call you to assemble on the parade ground for roll call. You may also be encouraged to rise by the gentle prod of German bayonets. You're to line up in columns of five. The Germans will count and compare the results to the number registered. If there are no discrepancies, this process will take only an hour or so."

He looked up from his notes before continuing.

"According to my RAF friends, the process may last several hours until there is an agreement on the numbers. Once there is, you will receive a cup of hot ersatz mint tea. For those of you who don't like the tea, you may want to use it to shave with because we don't have running hot water. In addition to the tea, each of you is limited to one cup of water per day."

The sergeant major paused as he shuffled his papers. No one spoke, waiting patiently for him to carry on.

"At 1100 hours you'll each receive a bowl of what the RAF call bed board soup. Apparently, it isn't made from bed boards, it just tastes like it. There may actually be some barley in it. Around 1500 hours the Germans will distribute your supper rations." He paused smiling. "By now you can probably guess it won't be your mother's cottage pie."

The men broke into laughter.

"Each group of six men will receive a loaf of German black bread made with rye grain, sawdust, leaves, straw, and sugar beets. You'll also get 3-5 boiled potatoes, depending on their size. Occasionally, the Germans will throw in a piece of cheese, and if you're lucky, it might be real cheese. There may also be some margarine or jam. Once a week you might get a small portion of German sausage or perhaps a small piece of fish."

The men looked at each other in disbelief wondering how they could possible survive on such meagre portions.

"I'll now draw your attention to a fact not realised by some in our previous world of plenty. The end slices of bread, potatoes, cheese, and sausages are smaller than those slices in the middle. The RAF pick one man in their group to cut the food into slices. They then draw to determine the order for selecting their slice. I suggest you do the same." He paused. "Any questions so far?"

"How the hell are we supposed to survive on that?" asked a Fusilier.

"I'm glad you asked," replied Beesley knowing he had the men's complete attention.

"At some point we'll begin receiving Red Cross Packages. According to the RAF, these packages are a godsend because they include food you'll need to survive," he said looking at the man who posed the question. "The allotment of the food needs to be managed carefully. The RAF band together in small groups they call muckers. Two, three, or four men share their food, clothing, and whatever else they may have. Sounds like another good idea."

A few men nodded their heads in agreement and gestured to friends.

"At 1600 hours roll call will be taken again then you'll be confined to your barracks until the next morning. The Germans will punish any man caught outside the barracks at night. They routinely patrol the compound with their Doberman Pinscher guard dogs once we're in for the night and occasionally they let the dogs loose without warning. These dogs are vicious so if you need to go to the latrine after lights out, be very careful."

Jean-Pierre looked over at Maurice who just shrugged his shoulders.

"Once a month you'll be marched to the bathhouse for 10 minute group showers while your mattresses are gassed with cyanide to kill the bed bugs and lice sharing your bed. You can write two letters and four postcards a month. You'll receive cartons of cigarettes. Even if you don't smoke, keep what you receive. Cigarettes are the camp's currency and the guards are eager to get their hands on real cigarettes. Apparently German cigarettes taste like shit."

"Serves the bastards right," muttered a POW. The sergeant major ignored the comment and continued.

"The RAF told me some of the guards are as the man just said, bastards. Do not provoke them. Though Germany is bound by the Geneva Convention in terms of how they treat prisoners of war, some guards are looking for any excuse to brutalise or kill POWs. If you noticed, a short wire runs parallel to the compound fence. The guards have orders to shoot anyone who steps over it, and they do. The RAF lost a couple of their chaps who intentionally or accidentally stepped over it."

Beesley's words echoed in Jean-Pierre's mind. He could not believe the Germans would shoot someone in cold blood for stepping over a wire. Sensing a need to lighten the mood amongst the men, Beesley changed subjects.

"For those of you corporals and higher who become bored, the job compound has postings for all sorts of work. Strange but it seems we have more non-commissioned officers now than when we left England."

The men laughed remembering his advice from Envermeu.

"There are hundreds of these working parties or Arbeitskommandos as they call them. Apparently there's work in factories, mines, quarries, sawmills, you name it they have it."

"I'm not working in a damn quarry. I'm a soldier not a labourer!" shouted one of the Canadians causing the other POWs to mumble their agreement.

"That's enough of that talk! Don't be so bloody high and mighty. I suspect before we're done here, you'll be doing many things a soldier normally wouldn't do."

The sergeant major turned over his last sheet.

"For those of you looking for less strenuous activities, the camp has a library you can use based on a schedule by compound. And thanks to our industrious neighbours, we'll be getting updates on the war's progress. They've constructed radio receivers from camp materials that tune in to the BBC."

He folded the papers and looked around the room.

"Things won't be pleasant here but it could be worse. There's a Soviet POW camp beside us and once in awhile you might see a wagon pulled by oxen. The wagon will probably be full of dead prisoners. The Germans dump their bodies in a pit in the nearby open field, cover them with lime, and a bulldozer fills in the hole.

There are some 30,000 Soviet POWs here. Some die each day from starvation, typhus, or their guards' brutality. The Geneva Convention doesn't cover them because the Soviet Union didn't sign the Convention. They don't have a Red Cross so they don't receive Red Cross packages. Most, if not all of them, will die here or at some other Stalag." He tucked his papers into his battledress pocket and looked at the men.

"That's it for now boys. It's been a bloody long day. We'll get through this together."

The sergeant major left the exhausted men to find their bunks and get some much-needed sleep.

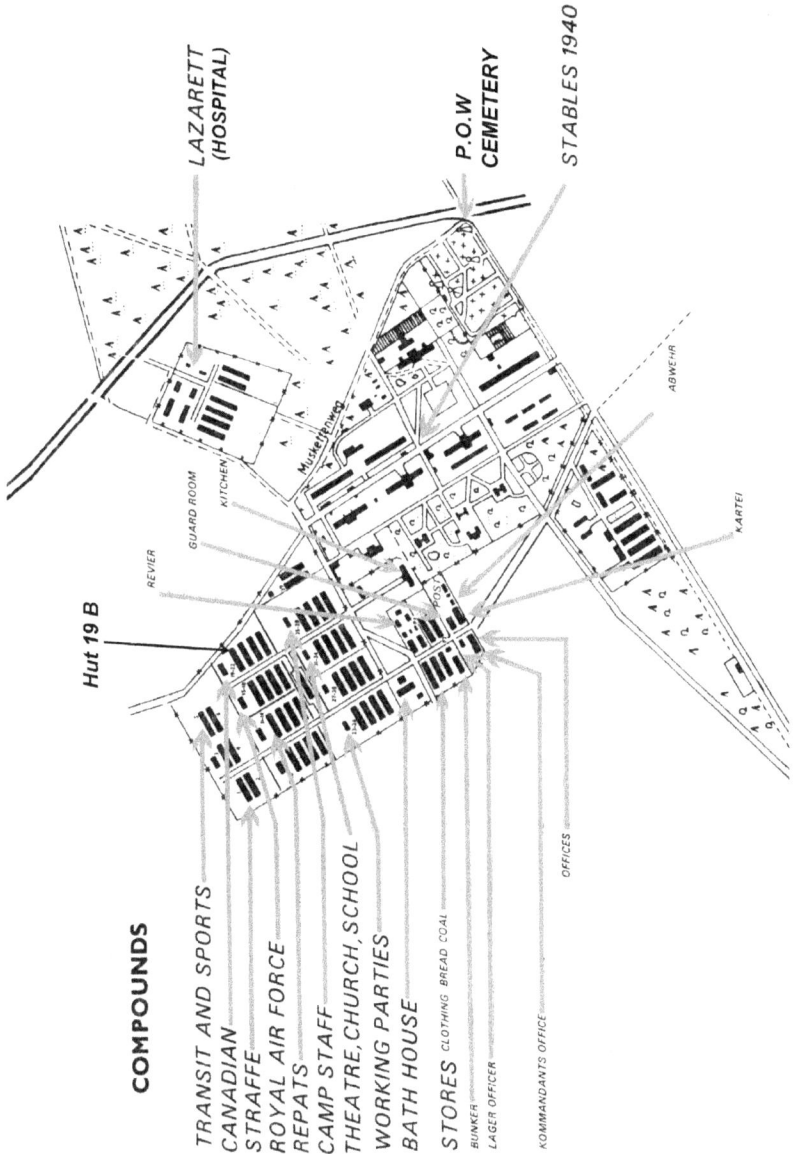

Plan of Stalag VIIIB, Lamsdorf, Germany. 1942. *Paul Juteau, Manuscript No.30.*

Chapter 22
Lamsdorf, Germany - Stalag VIIIB
Adapting
September 1942

Three days later, Jean-Pierre returned to the hospital.

"Well, well, well. You are a tough bird. A very lucky tough bird," said the doctor as he examined Jean-Pierre's hand. "Your thumb is responding well and the swelling is down. Most cases like yours end up with me removing the limb to prevent further loss or death. Only come back if the infection returns."

The good news failed to cheer up a downhearted Jean-Pierre. He never expected his quest for adventure to come to this, a wounded and humbled prisoner of war held in a camp deep within enemy territory, and cut off from the girl he loved. As he approached his barracks, Jean-Pierre caught sight of Maurice chatting with other POWs in the compound. He could not help laughing at the sight of his jovial friend walking awkwardly towards him.

"Where did you get those?" asked Jean-Pierre pointing to his friend's feet.

"The Germans found a pair to fit me," responded Maurice with a big grin as he looked down at his wooden clogs. "They aren't very comfortable and they cut into my ankles when I walk but it's better than going barefoot."

The two friends walked together, talked about the camp, and took comfort in each other's company. Jean-Pierre shared his thoughts and emotions with Maurice hoping to ease the burden of guilt he carried.

"Jean-Pierre, you know you did your best. You shouldn't feel guilty. If anyone should feel guilty, it's those idiots who organised the raid and believed it would succeed. We're going to get out of here. I don't plan to spend the rest of the war as a prisoner."

Weeks passed and Jean-Pierre gradually came to terms with his situation. Despite his wounds, he knew his condition did not compare with others in the hospital who suffered severe physical and mental ailments. He believed Maurice. Somehow, they would escape and he needed a sound body and mind to do so. Bolstered by Maurice's positive attitude, he set his objectives.

"I'll be ready when the time comes. While the warm weather is still with us, I'm going to walk, run, and do exercises. I'm going to play whatever sports they have. When I can't workout outside, I'll exercise in the barracks," he said to Maurice.

"What will you do? Use the bunks as an obstacle course?" Maurice laughed at Jean-Pierre's sincerity and passion for his new goal.

"Never mind. I will. What are you going to do to keep fit?"

"Don't worry about me Jean-Pierre. I was born fit."

True to his word, Jean-Pierre began to exercise and play sports. He also read books from the library, learned how to play chess, and studied German.

"When we get out of here, you'll be glad I can speak German."

"I'm not going anywhere until I get a pair of boots. Can you imagine me trying to outrun the Germans in these?" replied Maurice pointing to his weathered wooden shoes.

On 20 September, a month after their capture, the POWs received flimsy sheets of paper to write letters. In anticipation of a visit by the International Red Cross to inspect the newly arrived POWs and the state of their living quarters, the Germans gave each man just enough paper for two letters even though the Red Cross stipulated they could write two letters and four postcards each month

Jean-Pierre sat down in a quiet place to write a letter to his parents and one to Mary. Finally able to communicate with someone outside the camp boosted his morale and gave him a sense of freedom. The letter he wrote to his parents told them not to worry and he would write often. His tender letter to Mary contained heartfelt words of his love for her and the pain he felt because of their separation. When he finished writing her letter, he kissed her name, folded the paper, and put it in his blouse pocket until he could send it. Symbolically, a part of him would leave the camp with the letters.

Eight days later, a Red Cross delegation visited the camp to inspect the facilities for the new arrivals. They walked throughout the Canadian compound escorted by the camp commandant, German officers, and Sergeant Major Beesley. All appeared as it should. The Red Cross left a couple of volleyball nets and balls as well as a few soccer balls. They also brought baseball bats but the Germans later destroyed them while searching for secrets, weapons, or escape tools hidden inside. The Red Cross officials wrote up a favourable report, shared it with the camp commandant, and departed with the bundles of mail.

After six weeks of meagre rations, Jean-Pierre had lost 20 pounds. His clothes hung loosely on his gaunt frame but his body finally adapted to the reduced input and his weight loss stopped. At supper, he savoured the remains of his slice of black bread, visualising the feast he would order when released.

"When I get out, I'm going to have roast beef just like Mary's mother makes on Sunday," he said to Maurice. "There'll be two end pieces with a slightly burnt and crispy crust, some puffy, golden brown Yorkshire pudding, a mound of steaming mashed potatoes, and a serving of carrots. All covered with hot brown gravy made from the roast drippings."

"Right now I could go for a juicy hamburger and a plate of fries or perhaps a large serving of pâté chinois. I can see it on my plate with the steam rising from it," countered Maurice salivating. "Hell, I can even smell it."

Jean-Pierre put the last bit of bread in his mouth, closed his eyes, and tried to imagine the taste of roast beef.

"I can't believe the Germans give only this amount of food to their soldiers," commented a POW sitting beside them. "The Geneva Convention says they have to give us the same type and amount of food as they give their own troops. I think those buggers on the beach at Dieppe looked pretty well fed. What do you think?"

"I think you should file a complaint and see where it gets you, asshole," taunted a POW across the table tired of listening to never-ending discussions involving food.

The other man rose to the challenge.

"That's enough," a sergeant snapped as he stepped between the two antagonists. "You bloody well better remember what Beesley told you. You're soldiers in the bloody Canadian army and you damn well better act like soldiers. The Germans would like nothing better than for us to be at each other's throat but it's not going to happen. You understand?" he said glaring at one and then the other.

"Yes Sergeant," muttered the instigator as he walked away.

Stalag VIIIB with the Canadian compound in the background. *Imperial War Museum, HU_047094.*

Group photo of some of the occupants of Hut 19B. Stalag VIIIB, Lamsdorf, Germany. Jean-Pierre Laekas third row, 6th from the left. *I am Canada, Prisoner of Dieppe, Hugh Brewster, page 209.*

314 Catherine street north Hamilton

Regiment de Quebec

Pte Henri Alexandre Montreal
Pte Robert Alexandre Montreal
Pte Real Allard Montreal Pte
Paul Emile Archambault Montreal Acting L-Cpl Pierre Archambault, Montreal Pte. Roger Archambault Montreal Acting L Sgt.
Paul Arseneau Drummondville
Que Pte Gerard Aubry Terrebonne Pte Joseph Aubut Victoria
county N B Acting L-Cpl Lucien
Auclair Montreal Pte Gerard
Audet Montreal Pte Louis Audet
St Hermenegilde Que Acting L
Cpl Roger Audet Montreal Pte
Archill Auger address unknown
Pte Jean Barre Montreal Pte
Paul Emile Barrette Montreal
Pte Paul Barry, Mackayville Que
Pte Joseph Beaucage Montreal
Pte Albert Beauchamp Montreal
Pte Rolland Beauchamp Montreal
Acting L Cpl Antonio Beauden
Compton Que Acting Sgt Dena
Beaudoin Montreal Pte Laurent
Beaudoin Ste Christine Que Pte
Paul Emile Beaudoin Montreal
Pte Bernard Joseph Alph Beaudry Que Pte Aime Beaulieu
Montreal Pte Alexis Beaulieu
Rivere du Loup Que Pte Georges
Beaulne Lachine Que Pte Armand Beauvais, Montreal Pte
Roger Bedard Montreal Pte Roland Bedard Montreal Acting L
Sgt Julien Belair Montreal Pte
Leo Belisle Montreal Acting Cpl
Antonin Benjamin Montreal Pte
Sylvio Benjamin St Brigide Que
Pte Octave Benoit, Montreal Cpl
Paul Emile Benoit Montreal Cpl
Sylva Albert Benoit Montreal Pte
Edward Beresford St Therese
Que Pte Lorenzo Bernier Saya
bec Que Pte Leslie Bernicky,
Hawkesbury Ont Pte Florian
Bertrand Montreal, Pte Louis Bertrand Montreal Acting Cpl Roger
Berube Montreal Pte Adrien Bilodeau Montreal Acting Sgt Roland
Bilodeau Montreal Pte Gerard
Binette Montreal Pte Joseph Alphonse Bisson St Simon Les Mines
Que Pte Antoine Blais Montreal
Pte Roland Blais address unknown Pte Valere Blanchard Paquetville, N B Pte Marcel Blondon Montreal Pte Louis Boily,
Montreal Sgt Arthur Boivin Montreal Sgt Jean Baptiste Bock St
Jerome Que Pte Jean Paul Bonneau St. Jean, Que C Q M S Gilles
Bouchard Louisville Que Pte

Montreal Pte Henri Fontaine
Montreal Pte Wilfrid Fortin
Contre-Coeur Que Pte Marcel
Fournier Montreal Pte Arthur
Fraser Montreal Pte Paul Frigault Montreal Pte Jacques Fyfe
Montreal Acting L-Cpl Napoleon
Gagne Montreal Pte Arthur
Galarneau Montreal Pte Roland
Galarneau Montreal Acting L
Cpl Real Galipeau Granby Que
Pte Antonio Ganepy Ottawa
Acting L Cpl Patrick Gaudet
Montreal Pte Roger Gaulin,
Montreal Pte Leo Fortin, address
unknown Pte Georges Gauthier
Montreal Pte Jean Paul Gauthier
Montreal L-Sgt. Romeo Celinas
Laval County Que Pte Paul
Geoffrey Montreal Pte Rosaire
Genest St. Martin de Beauce Que
Pte. Raymond Geoffrion, Montreal Pte Emile Germain Montreal Pte Marcel Gervais address unknown Acting L Cpl
Georges Giguere Montreal
Acting L-Cpl Thomas Louis Gir
Montreal Pte Alphonse Gosselin
Halifax N S Pte Rosario Goulet,
Montreal Pte Francois Xavier
Gravel Joliette Que Pte Jean
Jacques Gravel Louiseville Que
Pte Jacques Grenier St Maurice
Que Pte Reginald Grenon Montreal Pte Georges Guerin Montreal L Cpl Louis Hamel Montreal Pte Roger Hamel, Montreal
Acting Sgt Claude Harrisson
Montreal Pte. Jean Hogue Montreal Pte Leo Houle Montreal
Cpl Joseph Guy Domina Yves
Huet Montreal Acting L. Cpl
Gaston Jalbert Cornwall Ont
Cpl Damasse Jette, Montreal Pte
Marcel Jolicouer Montreal Acting
Cpl Maurice Jolicoeur St. Vincent
de Paul Que Pte Guy Jolly
Montreal Pte Rene Jussiaume
Ottawa Pte Paul Juteau Montreal Pte Stephen Kelly Ste
Agathe des Monts Que Pte Walter Lyle Kendig, Armas, Kansas
Pte Marcel Labat, Montreal Pte
Jacques Labelle Iberville Que
Pte Leopold Labelle Montreal
Pte Romeo Laberge Montreal
Pte Roger Labrie Montreal Pte
Sylva Lacasse Montreal Pte
Henri Lacelle Montreal Pte
Jean Jacques Lachapelle Rouyn
Que Pte Alfred Ledouceur
St Jerome Que L-Cpl
Jean Pierre Laekas, Montreal
Acting Lance Cpl. Jean Marie Laferrier Bertherville Que Pte
Conrad Lafleur Masonville Que
Pte Aime Laframboise Montreal

Newspaper clipping from *The Hamilton Spectator* from Wednesday September 16, 1942 listing names of Canadians missing after the raid on Dieppe. Arthur Fraser, Maurice Jolicoeur, and Jean-Pierre Laekas are listed.

Chapter 23
Lamsdorf, Germany - Stalag VIIIB
Bound
October 1942–November 1942

On 8 October 1942, the POWs woke to find German machine guns on tripods and German soldiers surrounding the Canadian compound. They paraded out to roll call waiting for the German commandant to arrive. The atmosphere was tense as the Germans stared at them with stony faces. *They're going to execute us,* thought Jean-Pierre. The Germans took a group of POWs into one of the barracks. Jean-Pierre and his mates looked anxiously around for a way to escape if the Germans started shooting. At the sight and sounds of unrest among the POWs on the parade ground, the Germans cocked their weapons and prepared to fire.

The group of POWs exited the barracks with their hands tied. Again a murmur ran through the group, this time not so much from fear but from confusion as to the intent of their captors. After all the POWs had their hands tied, the German commandant addressed them.

"At the beach at Dieppe, we found the operational orders for your raid. They directed German prisoners' hands be bound which is in violation of the Geneva Convention. Furthermore, we also found the bodies of German prisoners at Dieppe with their hands tied. Your despicable treatment of German soldiers is inexcusable. As prisoners of war, those men were in your care. Those among you who carried out the orders have violated the terms of human decency proscribed in the international agreement signed by your country. Your actions deserve a punishment as brutal and cold as the act itself." He paused for effect and scanned the faces of the assembled POWs, as if searching for the culprits.

"It had been my intention to do so, but fortunately for you, der Fuehrer has intervened on your behalf. Your punishment is to remain tied until the British government acknowledges its responsibility for the crimes you have committed and apologizes for the shameful treatment of the brave Germans."

Back in the confines of the barracks, the men talked about their predicament.

"Even if you pay me, I ain't wiping your arse," said a Fusilier to one of his mates as they discussed how to manage different tasks with their tied hands.

"Well, who are you going to get to wipe yours?" responded his friend. "One of the German guards, perhaps?"

Although the POWs quickly figured out how to untie each other when the guards were not looking, Beesley submitted a formal complaint to the camp commandant. Four days later, the German officer spoke again to the assembled group of Canadians.

"The British government has not responded to our request, however, der Fuehrer has decreed your hands will be tied for only 18 hours a day."

Another formal complaint resulted in a further reduction to 12 hours a day, between 0800 hours and 2000 hours. The German government refused requests by Britain through the International Red Cross to cease the practice of tying the prisoners' hands. In response, the British government ordered the reciprocal tying of German prisoners' hands in allied POW camps.

In November, the temperature dropped and the first snow fell on the compound. The POWs were use to Canadian winters but as prisoners, they were ill prepared for the cold. A shortage of coal for the ovens left the barracks' interior uncomfortably chilly and most POWs wore the same summer battledress clothes they had at Dieppe. Jean-Pierre kept his clothes on when he went to bed, removing only his boots. His thin wool blanket provided little protection against the dampness around him.

He thought about Mary everyday since his letter and considered the possibilities why he had not heard from her. The doubts in his mind gnawed at him.

"Maurice, what if she was hurt or killed during the bombing in Brighton? What if she found someone else?"

"Jean-Pierre, calm down. I'm sure she's fine. I haven't received anything from Pierrette either so Mary's letter is probably on its way with all the others. If she really loves you, she'll write to you. If she found someone else, then it just wasn't meant to be."

Maurice's dispassionate response did little to ease Jean-Pierre's mind.

Towards the end of November, through the illicit camp radios, the POWs heard about the successful landings in North Africa. This brought much speculation about follow up landings in Europe and a quick end to the war.

"We'll be out of here before Christmas," announced an overly optimistic Fusilier.

"I'll bet you a package of cigarettes you'll be hanging your Christmas stocking in 19 B on Christmas Eve," responded his friend.

Mary's long awaited letter finally arrived on 26 November. After three months as a POW, Jean-Pierre was anxious to hear from the outside world, regardless of what the letter said. He unfolded it and laid it out on his bunk. He gazed at it for a moment not seeing the words but staring at Mary's handwriting. He could never mistake the left-handed slope of her unique writing style for someone else's. He read the introductory words and they warmed his heart. Then he stopped abruptly.

"We're going to have a baby?" he questioned aloud. Mary's words did not yet register in his mind. He re-read the letter. "We're going to have a baby," he yelled as the message became clear. *I'm going to be a father. We only made love once and we're going to have a baby,* he thought taking pride in his virile performance. He folded up the letter and raced out of the barracks looking for Maurice. Clutching the piece of paper in his bound hands and grinning from ear, he told everyone he passed the news.

"Maurice, I'm going to be a father!"

"Who's the mother?" asked Maurice with a sly grin.

"Mary of course, you idiot."

"Wonderful news, Jean-Pierre," responded Maurice with a broad smile on his face. "I know you'll be a great father. Congratulations."

"I have to write her a letter," said Jean-Pierre with a sense of urgency, "right away."

He turned and raced back to the barracks, leaving Maurice shaking his head and chuckling at Jean-Pierre's unrestrained joy. That evening, Jean-Pierre wanted desperately to send the letter but the next Red Cross visit was still weeks away.

The morning ritual of tying the men's hands with Red Cross parcel string ended on 2 December when the Germans replaced the string with a pair of manacles joined by a two-foot length of chain.

Manacles used on Canadian POWs. *Private Collection.*

Each morning, as they witnessed the ceremony, the RAF personnel in the adjoining compound heckled and jeered the German guards. After a few days, the Germans, tired of this belligerent reaction by the RAF, marched over to their compound and ordered the men to assemble. They shackled the RAF POWs but this lasted only a few days until the morning the RAF made a mockery of the process. Using the slotted keys from sardine cans, they managed to unlock the shackles. As quickly as a German guard manacled an RAF POW and moved on to do the next one, the prisoner unlocked his shackles then snuck back to the unshackled line of prisoners. The German officer in charge soon discovered what was going on. He threw his hands up in disgust, berated the guards, and ordered them to collect the manacles.

For 12 hours a day, the Canadians had to shave, eat, and use the latrines with their hands chained in front of them. Thanks to the RAF's keys, their lifestyle improved significantly, despite the risk of punishment if caught without their restraints. One day after roll call, Maurice returned to the barracks and began removing his shackles. With one hand free and the loose manacle swinging by the chain, Maurice looked up as a German SS guard entered the barracks. He looked at Maurice's free hand and motioned for him to exit. Maurice shrugged his shoulders, laughed, and casually approached the guard. The German pushed Maurice through the door.

"You little bastard," said Maurice as the guard marched him to the guardhouse, prodding him in the back with his rifle.

After conferring with the other guards, the SS soldier motioned for Maurice to stand at attention facing the guardhouse wall with his hands at his sides and his nose against the wall. Whenever Maurice moved or his nose left the wall, the guards struck him with their rifle butts. After an hour, the guards took Maurice to the low roll of concertina barbed wire near the Canadian barracks. Yelling at Maurice in German and gesturing, they forced him to strip. When he stood naked, they pulled him over to the wire, laid him on top of it, and tied his hands to the coils.

"So who's the little bastard now?" asked the SS guard in perfect English.

The guards admired their handiwork, laughed, and walked away. Four hours later, a smiling Maurice, with the manacles around his wrists, strolled back to the compound escorted by the SS guard.

Chapter 24
Lamsdorf, Germany - Stalag VIIIB
Red Cross Packages
December 1942

On 7 December, the Canadians' first delivery of Red Cross packages arrived. To Jean-Pierre, the sight of eager young men standing in the snow waiting for their packages could easily have been a picture on a Christmas card, if not for the barbed wire fences, the tall guard towers, and the armed German soldiers enviously watching the distribution.

"To establish a reserve of Red Cross packages in case of delays in future deliveries, we shall keep half of the packages, leaving one package for every two POWs," stated the German officer who supervised the process.

The guards resented the POWs receiving these parcels since the German government did not provide their own soldiers with any such luxuries. Consequently, they tried to restrict the allocation of the parcels without breaking the rules of the Geneva Convention.

Jean-Pierre and Maurice shared a package and took it back to the barracks. They stared for a moment at the battered cardboard box labelled with a large red cross and the words:

PRISONERS' PARCELS
THE CANADIAN RED CROSS SOCIETY
KRIEGSGEFANGENENPOST
COMITE INTERNATIONAL CROIX ROUGE,
GENEVE -TRANSIT. SUISSE

With deliberation, Jean-Pierre started opening the box.

"Come on Jean-Pierre. The bloody stuff will rot at the rate you're going."

They laid the box's contents on the bunk and stared in amazement at the abundance of food— butter, milk powder, cheese, corned beef, pork luncheon meat, salmon, sardines, dried apples, dried prunes, sugar, jam, hard biscuits, chocolate, salt, tea, and soap.

Once the Germans distributed all the parcels, the POWs talked and joked with one another, their spirits buoyed by the additional food. After three months of bed board soup and black bread, the men devoured most of the contents disregarding recommendations from their British neighbours to hoard their supplies.

After his arrival at Stalag VIIIB, Arthur became an active trader using the camp's currency of cigarettes. Though the Canadian Red Cross packages did not include tobacco, the POWs received plenty from the Canadian Army and their loved ones. Arthur traded cigarettes for goods, such as watches, rings, cigarette lighters, and any other items the men were willing to part with. He traded them for food then traded the food back for cigarettes, with each transaction bringing him a small profit. The Canadian Red Cross packages supplied Arthur with new investment capital for bartering. He took his cans of salmon to a barracks housing the Hindu POWs. As he prepared to enter, a Hindu soldier at the door stopped him.

"Where do you think you're going?"

"I have cans of salmon to trade."

"You can't come in now. We're eating and if you make a shadow over our food, we won't be able to eat it. Come back in half an hour when we're finished."

"I don't understand," replied Arthur confused by the man's explanation.

"Your shadow is impure because you're Chandalas. If it touches our food, we can't eat it."

Arthur shrugged his shoulders and left. He returned later with his tins of salmon.

"I've got salmon to trade," he said holding up his cans.

"How much do you want?" asked one of the POWs.

"Two cans of KAM for one can of salmon."

Once he finished with the Hindus, he went back to his barracks with his tins of KAM.

"Anyone want to trade some cigarettes for KAM?"

"How much do you want?"

"Fifty cigarettes for a can."

He went to a different barracks to trade his newly acquired supply of cigarettes for potatoes and bread. Moving through various barracks, he used the potatoes and bread to acquire more cigarettes.

"The whole process starts with the Hindus. They won't eat the pork in the KAM. It's useless to them which gives me leverage," he explained to a friend.

"What happens if they don't have KAM or anything else you want?"

"Then I go looking for Jewish POWs," responded Arthur matter-of-factly. "They won't eat the KAM either. But I only go to them as a last resort because they're much more difficult to deal with and I won't make as big a profit."

Jean-Pierre's first Christmas as a POW left him melancholy and sombre. The bitter taste of defeat still lingered. He attended the mass given by Padre Foote then retired to his hut for Réveillon. POWs in his hut, determined to make Christmas a celebration, hung decorations made of silver paper from cigarette packages and other scrounged materials. Their sparse meal consisted of food left over from Red Cross parcels. Maurice and Jean-Pierre enjoyed a small loaf of white bread obtained through a trade for cigarettes. After the sour German bread, the white bread tasted like cake. On Christmas day, the camp's theatre group performed a Christmas pageant. The festivities brought a pleasant change from the boredom of the daily camp routine, but they only temporarily brightened Jean-Pierre's outlook. To help raise his spirits, he joined a small group of Fusiliers walking around the camp singing French Christmas carols. As the day closed on his first Christmas as a POW, Jean-Pierre wondered where he would be for the next one.

Chapter 25
Lamsdorf, Germany - Stalag VIIIB
A New Year
January 1943-March 1943

The Fusiliers spent the New Year trying to stay warm. A POW responsible for Canadian logistics had ordered spare uniforms, boots, and great coats from the Canadian military shortly after their arrival at the camp in September but they received very little by the time the cold weather came. The men made do with clothes sent by their families or bought from the Germans using their cigarettes. Maurice still sported his clogs. Before venturing out in the snow, he stuffed the wooden shoes with the straw from his mattress to avoid frostbite. Winter storms kept the men indoors most of the time, except for trips to the latrine, cookhouse, and roll call. Bridge, chess, cribbage, card games, and books replaced the volleyball and soccer games. However, the large amounts of snow did bring the men some relief from the cold. It accumulated as high as the windows providing insulation against the frigid conditions.

Five months in captivity enabled the Canadians to develop an appreciation of the liberties they could take with their guards. Some guards respected the Canadians as fellow soldiers, while others looked for every opportunity to make the prisoners' lives miserable. The daily shackling continued but, over time, the more lenient German guards became less strict on the enforcement of Hitler's decree. On a particularly cold morning, one of the more likeable German sergeants entered Jean-Pierre's hut and told the men to assemble on the parade ground.

"Jesus Christ Fritz. We've done the roll call and we've got your handcuffs on," said a POW extending his manacled hands towards the German. "It's bloody cold out there."

"I have my orders. Believe me, I don't enjoy this anymore than you do. My orders are to conduct a random inspection of your bunks for illicit material, so please go outside. The faster you go, the faster you come back."

The German sergeant proceeded to the other section of the barracks with the same orders. Once emptied of POWs, the Germans conducted a detailed search of the men's bunks. With the inspection completed, the German sergeant "Fritz" went to the parade ground to dismiss the assembled POWs. He found them in formation in the prescribed columns of five, with each man wearing various types of winter garments. Their hands extended from the sleeves of their sweaters or coats with a shackle on each wrist linked by the chain. The German sergeant surveyed the group.

"You may now return to your huts," he said with a wry smile. "Would you like assistance in removing your coats and sweaters?"

"No thanks Fritz. We can manage."

Unlike Fritz, some of the other German guards took great pleasure in torturing their prisoners. One guard in particular enjoyed letting the Dobermans out at night to help patrol the compound. He would laugh at the sight of a POW scrambling back from the latrine chased by a vicious dog snapping at his heels. All the POWs feared the Dobermans and knew not to exit their huts after lights out unless they absolutely had to.

"Late last night, a Doberman caught and mauled someone on his way to the latrines," said Jean-Pierre meeting Maurice in the compound.

"Who?"

"I don't know his name but he was torn up pretty bad and died in hospital."

"Somehow we're going to get that bloody dog."

Maurice began planning how to avenge the soldier's needless death. He confided with the dead POW's friends and others who wanted the dog dead. All agreed with Maurice's plot and his offer to carry out the deed. A few nights later, the men heard the dog running loose in their compound. As planned, in barracks 22, furthest from the latrine, the POWs created a distraction that attracted the Doberman. Maurice crept to the latrine carrying an iron bar that he removed from his hut's stove. He carefully opened the door to avoid the squeaking of rusty hinges and, once inside, closed it just as carefully. Only the faint ambient lighting from the compound's tower lights along the fence and the searchlights' probing beams illuminated the latrine's interior. He felt his way along the wall counting his steps as he went. He stopped and bent down, sliding his hands down the wall. His fingers touched the ventilation screen frame. He tugged at the window-like structure until it came away from the wall, leaving a narrow opening just above the ground. He took sugar cubes from his pocket and placed one on the ground at the opening and others further inside the latrine. Satisfied with his arrangements, he waited. On schedule, the POWs in barracks 22 ceased their distraction. The dog, alerted by sounds coming from the front barracks, raced off. It stopped between barracks 19 and the latrine. A clucking sound coming from the latrine caught its attention and it ran towards the noise. The dog sniffed the air and followed the scent to the opening in the latrine wall. It snapped up the sugar cube and pushed its head through the opening to get another. More cubes lay just beyond its reach. As the dog forced its body into the narrow opening, Maurice brought the iron bar down with all his might across the back of the dog's neck. The dog died instantly and without a sound. Maurice and another POW dumped the 90-pound dog down a large drain. The Germans searched for the missing Doberman but never found it. That was the last time they sent a dog out alone into the compound.

Desperate to hear from Mary, Jean-Pierre wondered if she had already given birth and if she had, was it a boy as she predicted in her December letter. The Germans had not delivered any mail or Red Cross parcels for several months. Not only did the Red Cross packages help maintain their physical health but the books, clothing, and letters sent by the men's families, wives, and girlfriends provided emotional support. After many complaints regarding the lack of mail, Sergeant Major Beesley addressed the issue with the camp commandant.

"Permission to speak, sir?" said the sergeant major giving a smart salute.

"Permission granted."

"Sir, we haven't received any mail or Red Cross parcels for several months. Are they withheld for any particular reason?" asked Beesley implying the German's involvement in the delay.

The commandant smiled, removed his glasses, and rubbed the lenses with a handkerchief he drew from his pocket.

"Sergeant Major Beesley, the war has made things a little bit more difficult. The hold-up of your mail and Red Cross parcels is most likely due to bombing by British and American planes of the rail lines used by Sweden and Switzerland to bring the material to us. I can assure you I have not ordered a stoppage in the distribution of either parcels or mail."

News from the POWs' illicit radio sets confirmed the commandant's assessment of the delay. The men were pleased with the Allies advancement but it came at the expense of the parcels that sustained them. It was another two months before the POWs received mail. Jean-Pierre received two letters in March, one from his father, and one from Mary. As much as he wanted to open Mary's first, he also wanted to savour the moment, read and then re-read her letter. He opened his father's, smiled as he read its contents, and then moved on to Mary's letter. He picked it up, opened it carefully, and read her words. She gave birth on 5 February to a healthy boy by the name of Michael John, the names of Jean-Pierre's father, and Jean-Pierre's English equivalent. Jean-Pierre stared at the letter and tears of joy formed in his eyes.

"My son," he whispered to himself. His forearms broke out in goose bumps and a shiver ran up his back. "My son," he repeated quietly.

He ran off to find Maurice.

"Maurice, I'm a father. I have a son," he shouted to his friend.

"I'm very happy for you, my friend. You'll have a handsome little boy waiting for you when we get out of here."

"But Maurice, what if we don't?"

Maurice could see the concern on his friend's face.

"What if we don't?" he repeated.

"Jean-Pierre, don't worry. I promise you'll see him."

Distribution of Red Cross packages at Stalag VIIIB at Lamsdorf 1943. *Courtesy of the Red Deer and District Archives mg-332-2-13.*

Chapter 26
Lamsdorf, Germany - Stalag VIIIB
Escapes
April 1943–November 1943

The POWs came from all walks of life including artists, musicians, actors, tailors, policemen, businessmen, lawyers, barbers, shoemakers, butchers, teachers, bakers, construction workers, and miners. This diverse and talented group shared and worked towards a common interest, how to make their confinement a little more bearable and to help with escapes. Not long after arriving in Stalag VIIIB, Sergeant Major Beesley consulted with the British POWs and established a Canadian escape committee. The committee chose hut 19B as the location for the entrance to the tunnel, since it was only 100 feet from the wire fence. They created a trap door under one of the bunks and digging started before the first snowfall. Winter prevented the work from continuing because the excavated dirt would not easily blend in with the frozen earth of the compound, particularly when it snowed. With the arrival of spring, escape activities were in full force. To support the tunnelling effort, each Canadian POW donated two bed boards for shoring in the tunnel.

"Shit!" exclaimed a Fusilier as a committee member removed another bed board. "How the hell do you expect me to sleep on what you've left me?"

"Take the cord from your Red Cross package and make a net, just like everyone else," replied the POW.

In addition to bed boards, the Canadians used whatever they managed to get their hands on for the tunnel. Empty tins of powdered milk, prisoners' kit bags, and stolen hockey sticks made a ventilation system. Homemade lamps with cloth wicks soaked in margarine provided light. Pieces of scavenged metal made tools. They also bought materials from guards they trusted. To dispose of the excavated earth, volunteers carried the dirt in long sausage-like bags running down the inside of their pant legs. As they walked around the compound or watched volleyball and soccer matches, they released small amounts and used their feet to blend it in with the compound's earth. Other hiding places included a vegetable garden and the latrine.

"I volunteered to go down and dig. I stuck it out as best I could but it was much too confined for me," said Maurice as he and Jean-Pierre strolled around the perimeter of the compound, dispensing earth from their trouser legs.

"They have ex-miners doing most of the critical work," replied Jean-Pierre. "It's pretty dangerous down there. If you're not careful the roof could cave in." Maurice stopped and took off his wooden clog to remove a pebble lodged in his shoe, no doubt from the tunnel.

"I'm surprised a big lug like you could even fit down there."

"With a bloody opening of two square feet, I thought I would suffocate."

They continued shuffling their feet around the compound spreading the dirt with the other POWs.

"Are you planning to get out through the tunnel?" asked Jean-Pierre.

"The committee told me I needed to speak German. I'm making my own plans. Do you want to join me?"

Jean-Pierre hesitated in responding and Maurice knew what Jean-Pierre's answer would be.

"Maurice, I can't afford to take any unnecessary chances. Mary and my son ...."

"Don't worry Jean-Pierre. In your situation I would do the same."

In the summer of 1943, Maurice received a pair of boots. After a year of wearing the wooden clogs, the boots felt like slippers. Though worn, they protected his feet and gave him the mobility that the clogs could not. He wasted no time in planning his escape. He decided his chances might be better if he left the camp as part of a work group. At the work compound, he found a job for the next day that involved travelling to a distant quarry to mine chalk. Unfortunately, no openings remained but he met up with a member of the work party. An Australian POW agreed to switch identities with him. The following morning, Maurice boarded the truck with other POWs from his compound. He recognised two as British Marine Commandos.

"Were you captured at Dieppe?" asked Maurice.

"Sure enough, at Berneval. No. 3 Commando. What about you?" asked the marine noticing Maurice's Canada patch on his shoulder.

"On the main beach right in front of their bloody guns."

In the ensuing discussion, the marines learned Maurice fought with their battalion at Vågsøy Island, Norway. In their eyes, this revelation made Maurice a brother in arms.

"We're planning on getting out while we're at the quarry. Want to join us?" whispered the commando.

Maurice nodded affirmatively. When the truck arrived at the quarry, the Germans gave the POWs picks and shovels then led them in small groups to their work area. That evening, the Germans put the men in a barracks located not far from the quarry, padlocked the door from the outside then retired for the evening to their own quarters. The marines and Maurice walked over to one of the windows and surveyed their situation.

"I hadn't expected bars on the windows," said Maurice as he gripped two metal rods and attempted to move them.

"Not to worry mate. When the time comes, the bars won't be a problem."

The commandos spent the next two days and nights monitoring the guards' movements.

"We're going tonight. The Germans don't bother with us after lights out and there are plenty of clouds to block the moonlight."

That evening one of the commandos produced a hacksaw blade and a small container of machine oil. While he attended to the bars, the other commando and Maurice tore strips from their blankets. They wrapped them around their feet to help muffle the sound of their boots on the stony courtyard. The rest of the work party looked on disinterestedly. They did not intend to join in. This was not the first escape they witnessed and would probably not be the last.

"That's it. Let's go," said the marine as he removed the last bar.

They squeezed through the window then sprinted across the courtyard to the nearby woods. Maurice turned to see if the Germans had seen or heard them. No one stirred. Their mutually agreed objective was neutral Switzerland. Heading in a southwesterly direction, they travelled with great care at night and sought shelter before daybreak in secluded areas. Though they brought food and water with them, they stole vegetables from gardens at every opportunity to maintain their own supplies. They refilled their water containers from running brooks and streams. One day, they jumped on a freight train that seemed to be heading in the right direction until it slowed on the outskirts of a town. Fearing detection if the train stopped in the town, they jumped off and continued on foot, giving the town a wide berth. Twenty-five days later, they rested on the banks of a river, sheltered in dense bush. The lead commando consulted a map and small compass.

"That's the Bregenzer Ach," he whispered pointing to water. "We're in Austria and over there beyond those hills, is the Swiss border, probably 10 or 11 miles away. We just need to find a place to cross."

"It doesn't look very wide," responded Maurice in a hushed voice. "We could swim across." He gazed at the distant hills. *I'm almost there. Just 11 more miles.*

"I can't swim," said the second commando.

"What do you mean?" exclaimed Maurice.

"I can't swim. You two go on and I'll find a way."

"I'm not bloody well leaving you here after we've come this far," said his mate.

"Let's look for an unguarded bridge to cross," offered Maurice knowing he could not desert his two comrades.

They spent the day resting with one on watch while the other two slept. As the sun slipped below the horizon, the anxious men prepared to leave their shelter. They cautiously walked towards a road that followed the river.

"Halt!"

The command shattered the stillness. The three men froze. The familiar shapes of German army helmets appeared from the woods as the patrol approached. With no chance to escape, the three fugitives surrendered.

Following Maurice's departure from the camp, Jean-Pierre met some members of the Calgary Tanks who spoke German. He told them he wanted to learn to speak German well enough to carry on conversations. They agreed to help in exchange for Jean-Pierre teaching them some French. In addition to the time he spent with the Calgarians, Jean-Pierre attended formal classroom sessions given by German-speaking British soldiers. Jean-Pierre filled his days with German instruction, sports, exercise, card games, and writing letters to Mary.

One afternoon, Jean-Pierre noticed his friend's familiar shape approaching the parade ground escorted by a German guard.

"What happened?" asked Jean-Pierre once the guards had left.

"We were almost in Switzerland. Then we got caught. They beat us up pretty good."

"Who's we?"

"Me and two British commandos. They sent us to Kraków in Poland and the SS there had a go at us before sending us back here. I just finished 30 days in solitary confinement."

"Are you okay?"

"I'm fine." He paused for a moment. "Jean-Pierre, it was so close I could smell it," he said shaking his head. "So what have I missed while I was away?"

"Not too much. My son and Mary are fine. Our camp was renamed Stalag 344 and I've got a job as an interpreter for our compound."

"You speak German that well?"

"You would too with two months of intensive training."

"Well, well. You have been a busy little beaver."

"Speaking of beavers, the march of the penguins came to an end last week."

"March of the penguins?"

"You know, all of us waddling about the compound like penguins and spreading the excavated dirt. The tunnel is finished."

"That won't help me get out of here." He looked at Jean-Pierre with an air of determination. "You can't imagine the feeling of being so close. I'll keep trying until I make it."

During the digging of the tunnel, some sports events such as soccer and volleyball matches were arranged by the escape committee to permit spectators to dispose of tunnel earth as they mingled on the sidelines. However, some POWs were sports enthusiasts and organised inter-compound events for the pure joy of competition. These included soccer, volleyball, baseball, and boxing matches as well as track and field.

While watching a baseball game, Maurice discussed his new plans with Jean-Pierre.

"Don't be surprised when you don't see me tomorrow," he warned his friend. "There's a work party leaving to load food supplies on trains and I put my name down to go."

"Be careful and try not to get caught this time," replied a concerned Jean-Pierre.

Not long after Maurice left, 40 Canadian POWs escaped from Stalag VIIIB using the tunnel. Two made it safely to Sweden. Jean-Pierre's fluency in German might have earned him a spot, but he turned down the offer to participate. The Germans only learned of the escape days later when the camp's commandant received a humiliating message from the SS. They told him of the capture of a large group of Canadian POWs who claimed to be from Stalag 344. The commandant called for the additional German soldiers and armoured cars stationed nearby. The Germans assembled the Canadians in the compound and began a meticulous roll call under the watchful eyes of armed guards. In the meantime, German soldiers stormed through the barracks turning over bunks and thumping the floor to sound for cavities. They eventually discovered the tunnel. While the Canadians waited assembled on the parade ground, German soldiers rigged the tunnel with explosives and blew it up, throwing a column of earth into the air.

"Three cheers for our tunnel," shouted a Canadian POW as the dust began to settle. "Hip, hip."

"Hooray," came the rousing chorus from the assembled POWs.

"Hip, hip."

"Hooray."

"Hip, hip."

"Hooray."

Arthur also had plans to escape. He too chose work parties as his way. From his experience bartering for cans of salmon, he met some Palestinian Jewish POWs who worked in the coalmines every day. Arthur and a few other Fusiliers arranged to change identification tags and barracks with the Palestinians. In the morning, Arthur and the other Fusiliers left the camp with the labour party. When they arrived, the work party leader pulled Arthur and his friends aside and offered them a cup of ersatz coffee.

"I'm Jewish," said the man to Arthur, "but I can tell you're not. What are you up to?"

"We're planning to escape and we want to make contact with a Polish civilian to help us."

"For a price, I can arrange it."

The men gave him a package of cigarettes and he put them to work with a group of Polish prisoners. The dangerous underground work involved digging coal and filling small wooden coal carts. The carts travelled on a narrow gauge track that ran from the depths of the mine back to the surface. The Germans set a daily quota of 16 carts of coal for the group. Initially Arthur took it easy, not wanting to contribute to satisfying the German's need for coal. The work was hard and dirty and there was the ever-present danger of stones falling from the mine's unsupported ceiling. He soon realised the Polish labourers had to make up for his shortcomings in productivity to meet the German's daily quota. Arthur increased his output. The malnourished Poles received no food during the day. Arthur stopped bringing sandwiches to work because he could not bear to see the look on the Poles' faces as they watched him eat. Days passed with no indication when they would meet with a Polish civilian to help with their escape. Arthur complained to the Jewish leader who took their cigarettes. The next day, German soldiers took Arthur and the other Fusiliers back to Stalag VIIIB. A German officer charged them with attempting to escape and gave them each one week in solitary confinement. As they locked him in his cell, it was clear to Arthur how the Germans found them out. *If they want any more bloody cans of salmon from me, it's going to cost them.*

On 21 November 1943, the Germans finally discontinued shackling the Canadians. The Swiss managed to convince the stubborn Germans and British politicians to put aside their squabble in the interest of easing conditions for their respective soldiers in POW camps. After 13 months with his hands bound, Jean-Pierre thought it strange the first few mornings when he did not have to line up for the chaining ritual.

In early December, Jean-Pierre met Maurice returning once more to the compound escorted by a German guard.

"Jean-Pierre, you won't believe it. I ended up in Odessa on the Black Sea." He laughed at the absurdity of his comment.

"How the hell did you get there? The place must have been crawling with Krauts."

"When I left here, they took us to Szolnok, Hungary. There was a huge warehouse full of sacks of flour. We worked for a few days just turning the sacks over so they wouldn't get damp. The sacks were all stamped with the date of 1919!"

"From the First World War?"

"Yes. That flour has been there for over 20 years. Someone must have been turning the sacks all that time."

"But how did you get to Odessa?"

"Well, a train arrived and we had to load it with the flour. On one of my sack carrying trips, I found a good hiding place in a boxcar and stayed there. A couple of days later, the train stopped at the port of Odessa and they began unloading. I tried to blend in with the Russian prisoners but I must've stood out like a sore thumb with my Canadian uniform."

"Then what happened?" asked Jean-Pierre intrigued with his friend's adventure.

"The Krauts locked me in a cell. The next day, they interrogated me while a couple of guards beat me up. They didn't believe I escaped from Stalag 344 I guess because it's so far away. They let me know they weren't too pleased to see me. When they finished, they made me walk for seven days until we reached Yugoslavia. From there we took the train and here I am."

"Well at least they didn't shoot you. I'm glad you made it back alive."

"I'm not giving up Jean-Pierre. At the next opportunity, I'm going to try again."

Jean-Pierre smiled and shook his head, amazed by his friend's unrelenting pursuit of freedom. Sergeant Major Beesley had told them it was their duty as soldiers to escape and fight again. Maurice, the consummate soldier, took that duty seriously.

Sports at Stalag VIIIB with soldiers in background. *Canadian War Museum, 19740246-013, Photo Archives T 1.10, Image #6.*

Stalag VIIIB boxing match. *Library and Archives Canada, Thomas W. McLean POW Collection, Archival reference no. R778-1-1-E, File # 1 [29], e010797101-v8.*

Chapter 27
Lamsdorf, Germany - Stalag 344
Goodbye
December 1943–January 1944

As they approached their second Christmas at Stalag 344, Jean-Pierre believed the tide of war now favoured the Allies. BBC broadcasts announced the German's devastating defeat at Stalingrad, the surrender of Axis troops in North Africa, the Allies landing in Sicily, and Italy's armistice with the Allies. Allied aircraft continued to bomb German industries and cities by day and night. *It won't be long now before we're freed*, he thought.

Just before Christmas, he received a letter from Mary with a picture of her holding his son. He stared at the picture and started crying. Mary looked so beautiful and there was his 10-month-old son smiling, without a care in the world. He wanted so much to be with them. He quickly looked around to see if anyone noticed his tears as he wiped them away. After kissing the picture, he put it in the breast pocket of his blouse close to his heart.

Christmas Eve was much like their previous one. Their homemade decorations once again adorned the barracks. Jean-Pierre went to mass with other Fusiliers and then he returned to his barracks for Réveillon. On their ingeniously designed blower stoves, the designated chefs prepared meals from their combined hoarded supplies. Jean-Pierre dined on mashed potatoes with roasted canned pork and gravy. For dessert, he enjoyed a pudding made with biscuits, powdered milk, and dried fruit. On Christmas Day Jean-Pierre joined a group of Fusiliers singing their favourite French Christmas carols as they strolled around the compound. Later that day as he watched actors performing a Christmas pageant, he overheard a nearby discussion between two POWs.

"You want to hear the latest? We're leaving after Christmas. In January, they're sending us to a place called Stargard close to the Baltic Sea."

"Why?"

"How the hell do I know? It's probably because of all our escape attempts."

In fact, the Germans had decided to transfer British and the Canadians prisoners to other POW camps to offset the continuing influx of new POWs to Stalag 344 and to address the growing health concerns. Inadequate supplies of coal to heat the barracks left the men searching continually for other combustible materials. Even the latrines' wooden seats had been used for firewood. The increased demands on the camp's water supply reduced the already limited amount available to each POW for drinking and washing. The waste collection crew could not empty the latrines quickly enough to keep up with the increased excrement accumulating.

Sure enough, early in the New Year, the Germans notified Sergeant Major Beesley of the upcoming transfer of Canadians to Stalag IID. They told him he would not be accompanying them. Hearing the news, some of the men felt ill at ease, having grown accustomed to the place, their sergeant major, and the camp routine. After almost 18 months of captivity, Stalag 344 had become their home.

On 26 January 1944, the Canadian POWs lined up on the parade ground. They marched in formation through the compound towards the front gates. In their packs, they carried their personal effects including cigarettes, food, extra clothes, and other prized possessions. Jean-Pierre kept Mary's letters in the pocket of his battle dress, not trusting the security of her cherished notes to his tattered haversack. As he exited the camp, Jean-Pierre took one last look back. He remembered the day he arrived, wounded in body and spirit, wondering how he would survive. The 18 months at Stalag 344 had transformed him into a hardened and experienced survivor.

I'm still a Fusilier and will always be until this damn war is over. They marched down Chestnut Alley, past the cemetery, and down the road to the railway halt where they had arrived on 3 September 1942. The line of wooden boxcars stood waiting for them. They began boarding, crowding in to the small enclosures. Unlike their last experience, this time they welcomed the press of their bodies for the warmth it provided in the bitter cold. Inside the car, he stamped his feet to remove the snow clinging to his boots. As German soldiers pulled the door shut, Jean-Pierre did not feel the same sense of panic he had on their first train journey. *The next bloody camp can't be any worse than this one. Besides, the way the war is going, we won't be there long.*

Chapter 28
Stargard, Germany - Stalag IID
A New Home
January 1944–May 1944

The 400-mile journey from Stalag 344 took three days. On 29 January 1944, the Canadians disembarked at the Stargard train station, relieved to leave the crowded boxcars behind. The POWs marched from the train station along snow-covered streets towards Stalag IID, one mile away. Wounded German soldiers, some wearing tattered clothing, walked wearily beside them headed in the same direction.

"That's probably the way we looked walking through Dieppe," said the Fusilier marching next to Jean-Pierre as they surveyed the sorry looking lot of German soldiers.

Jean-Pierre called out to one of the German guards escorting the Canadians. Without stopping, he gave the guard a cigarette. The guard kept pace with Jean-Pierre while they conversed in German for several minutes. Then the guard nodded and walked away.

"How in the hell do you know German?" asked the Fusilier.

"I picked it up during my spare time over the last year and half." He gestured with his head towards the wounded Germans. "They're from the Russian front. They've been sent to Stargard for treatment at the military hospital. The guard figures there are about 30,000 wounded in the barracks near the hospital. As soon as they're fit, they'll be sent back."

"Thirty thousand?"

"Yeah. He said the Russians are kicking the shit out of the German army. He thinks the war is lost and he's hoping he won't be sent back to the front."

"Christ. If the Germans think the war is over then we should be out of here in no time."

Jean-Pierre smiled at the thought.

The Germans claimed Stalag IID to be a model POW camp. Built at the start of the war in 1940, it included modern barracks, a revier or medical station, and a large military hospital close to the camp. It housed only 18,000 POWs but served as a staging centre for work parties. Over 200 work parties originated from the camp providing labour to the area's farms and industries. Many of the work parties operated in remote locations with the POWs billeted in barracks or other facilities at the work site. In most cases, this resulted in improved living conditions for the prisoners.

It was not by chance the Germans transferred the Canadians to Stalag IID. The International Red Cross had reported the excellent treatment of German POWs in camps across Canada and German POWs also acknowledged this in their letters home. The German authorities reciprocated by transferring the Canadians to one of their best camps.

As Jean-Pierre marched through the gates, he compared his surroundings to his previous home. Guard towers overlooked the camp and, once inside, barbed wire fences enclosed the site. *I guess they're all the same,* he thought. *Except this one seems smaller than VIIIB and there are no Dobermans waiting to greet us.* The guards led them to three grey, low-level, stone buildings in a compound that housed other barracks. Each barracks accommodated 300 men. Inside the barracks, the familiar rows of three-tier wooden bunks greeted Jean-Pierre but he noticed a significant difference in the barracks' central area. He counted 26 water taps for washing. *Things are looking up.* After almost 18 months in captivity, he knew the drill and soon settled in. Unlike their previous camp, the Canadians found themselves sharing their barracks and compounds with various nationalities: New Zealanders, Australians, British, Yugoslavs, Greeks, and Frenchmen. Although the Germans did not transfer Sergeant Major Beesley to Stalag IID, another non-commissioned officer, Sergeant Major Liscombe of the Essex Scottish, took charge of the men. The men's daily routine mirrored that of Stalag 344 except for the relaxed discipline. Most of their German guards were veterans of the Russian front and respected the POWs as soldiers.

Stalag IID, Stargard, Germany. *Author unknown.*

"I can't say I enjoy being a POW, but if I had a choice I would prefer to stay here than any other camp until the war ends," proclaimed a Canadian POW several weeks after their arrival. "Can you believe it? We get three hot showers a week!"

"You wouldn't say that if you were a Russian POW. I really don't understand why the Germans have to be so hard on them," countered his bunkmate.

"Do you remember when the Germans gave us some copies of Hitler's Mein Kamp in VIIIB?"

"Yeah. I found you needed two pages together to wipe your ass and not have your finger break through."

"Well I started reading each page before I wiped."

"How bloody enlightening and efficient."

"In response to your question, I believe the answer is in his book."

"Do tell."

"Hitler wanted the land east of Germany to settle and feed the expansion of his master race. He regarded the Slav inhabitants as subhuman only worthy of deportation to Siberia or slave labour. He planned to annihilate them all. This is the ideology he preached in his book and is carried out here in the camps."

"If the Russians get the upper hand, there'll be a terrible settling of accounts."

"It has already started on the Russian front. Our guards are deathly afraid of being sent there."

"How do you know that?"

"I forgot his name but a Fusilier told me. He speaks German and talks to the guards regularly."

Fortunately for the men, Padre John Foote was among the Canadian contingent sent to Stalag IID. He wasted no time in starting his nondenominational church services each Sunday. In addition to attending to the men's spiritual needs, Padre Foote also helped organise various activities to take their minds off the apparent hopelessness of their situation.

During the frigid winter months, the POWs received a special surprise. The city of Calgary sent their namesake Tank battalion a full set of hockey equipment. The Germans permitted the POWs to build a small ice rink and watched in amazement as the Canadians raced up and down the rough surface chasing a small, hard rubber disk. As in Stalag 344, the Canadians' ability to maintain high spirits and adapt to prison camp life puzzled the German guards.

Early spring rains washed away the ice rink and snow turning the compound into a quagmire, until a week of clear weather and winds dried up the mess. Volleyball nets replaced hockey nets and a new sports season began. The camp's large sports field provided enough space for the men to play soccer, baseball, cricket, and rugby.

The Red Cross finally received notification of Stalag VIIIB's new name of 344 but by then most of the Canadians had already transferred to Stalag IID. The Germans provided the Red Cross with the list of relocated Canadians and eventually the Red Cross packages, cigarettes, and mail from loved ones found their way to Stalag IID. Bartering again occupied a good part of the men's time.

Maurice acquired a camera from a German guard for the price of a package of cigarettes. To assist with escapes, he photographed soldiers for their identity papers. The camp's Italian dentist, captured by the Germans after Italy's surrender, developed the photographs.

"Jean-Pierre," called Maurice from across the compound. "I want a photo of the two of us so I can remember what the camp looks like."

"Where do you think you're going?"

"I told you I'm not hanging around here waiting for the war to end. There's a work party that goes off every morning to dig up stumps and tree roots for firewood."

"So?"

"According to my sources, the train tracks to Stettin are close to the work party's site. Stettin is on the Baltic Sea so if I can jump a freight headed that way, then all I need is a boat to Sweden."

"Jesus, Maurice. Don't you remember what happened the last couple of times you tried to escape?"

"You can't change my mind, Jean-Pierre. I'm volunteering for that bloody work party then I'm getting a reservation on a boat to Sweden. Now get over here so we can have our damn picture taken."

The next morning Maurice went off with the work party. They walked in the direction of Stargard and within 30 minutes reached their destination. A mess of unsightly stumps covered a large barren field. A stand of tall pines stood nearby, still untouched by the workers' saws and axes. As he struggled with other POWs to extract the tangled and twisted tree roots from the earth, he surveyed his surroundings. Railroad tracks ran by the field and disappeared behind the pines. The two guards assigned to the work party chatted with one another, completely ignoring the POWs. Trains passed by at regular intervals heading towards Stettin, all of them pulling freight cars. Maurice made mental notes for his escape plan. Dirty, hot, and tired, the POWs stopped late in the afternoon when a horse-drawn wagon appeared. They loaded their day's work onto the wagon then started walking back to the camp. The guards led the POWs to the Stargard train station allowing them to use the station's lavatories. As Maurice came out of the latrine, he wandered past the unoccupied stationmaster's office. He glanced over his shoulder. Seeing no one, he darted into the office his eyes quickly scanning the room. A stamp sat on an ink pad on the desk. He quickly pocketed it then rejoined the work group sitting on the front steps. When he returned to camp, he approached a member of the escape committee.

"Here's a little something you could use," he said holding in the palm of his hand an official German travel stamp emblazoned with the Nazi swastika. "In return, I need some help getting the hell out of here."

The escape committee member nodded his head and beckoned Maurice to follow him to his barracks. They joined a group of POWs seated at a table. Most of them knew Maurice from his previous escape attempts.

"What's up Maurice?" asked the group's leader.

Maurice handed him the stamp.

"Very nice," said the leader examining the stamp's markings. "I suppose you would like something in return?"

"I need some help getting out of here."

"Well now, sit down and tell us how we can be of assistance."

Jean-Pierre's knowledge of German served him well. Several German guards at the camp took a liking to the young French Canadian who conversed with them in their own language. Jean-Pierre made the most of this relationship and traded cigarettes in return for the opportunity to accompany the guards on occasional daytrips to Stargard.

"I'm off to town Maurice. Can I get you get anything?" taunted Jean-Pierre as he prepared to leave on one of his excursions.

"Yes. Bring me back a hamburger and a pint of beer, you bastard."

Jean-Pierre laughed and walked to the guard's hut. He put on a civilian greatcoat to wear over his uniform and a fedora. For a few extra cigarettes, he also received some German-issued Polish currency. Later that day when Jean-Pierre returned to the compound, Maurice noticed the concerned look on his friend's face.

"What's wrong Jean-Pierre? Did you eat too many donuts?"

"I don't think I'll be making the trip to town anymore?"

"Why not?"

"I went to the usual café and ordered a blackcurrant tea and a pączki. I sat at my regular spot watching people come and go. A German officer came in, bought a tea, and sat at the table next to mine."

"Was he from the camp?"

"I don't know. I didn't recognise him."

"So what happened?"

"He took out a cigarette and asked, 'Do you have a light?' I told him I didn't."

"Did he speak to you in Polish or German?"

"German of course! Then he said, 'It's a beautiful spring day.' I agreed and said something like the buds were already out on the trees."

"Damn. I wish I could speak German like you. And then what happened?"

"He got up and said, 'I trust you will be able to find your way back to the camp,' in perfect English."

"Shit."

"I told the guards on the way back and they said my trips to Stargard are over. They're worried their next trip might be to the Russian front."

In the late spring, Arthur signed up to work at a sub-camp located on a vegetable farm. The Germans established 20 such labour camp detachments all around Germany, exclusively for the Canadians. Based on feedback from friends, Arthur knew these camps provided the POWs with access to food and he looked forward to a change of scenery.

"One of the guards told me we're going to replace a group of French POWs on a huge vegetable farm run by a German Nazi," said a Fusilier sitting beside Arthur in a German transport truck.

"Great. I just love working for the Nazis. How about you?" responded Arthur sarcastically.

They arrived at an expansive farm late in the afternoon near the town of Leipzig. Two large wooden barracks sat in a small fenced-in compound overlooking the farm and a small village below. The whitewashed buildings looked in desperate need of repair. The men entered the barracks then stopped in their tracks.

"This is worse than Verneuil," said Arthur in disgust.

"I'm not sleeping in this filth," exclaimed a POW as he stormed out.

The work group, consisting of about 40 Canadians, agreed they would be much better off in their barracks at the camp. They asked the guards to take them back. A stern faced and slightly balding man approached the group. He wore brown riding breeches, knee-high brown leather boots, and a grey blazer with the Nazi party pin in his lapel. He walked with a limp, his weight supported by a cane.

"Damn Canadians!" he exclaimed in German upon hearing of their complaint from the guard. He raised his cane to strike a POW. The Canadian ripped the cane from the Nazi's grip as the other POWs quickly surrounded him. The guard calmed the POWs then turned to the incensed German.

"You can't do that. You're a civilian and they're soldiers. If you hit a soldier, something bad may happen to you."

The Nazi looked at the guard in disbelief.

"These Canadians are very special prisoners. You're not allowed to touch them."

The farm owner pushed past the Canadians and stormed off to the large house at the end of the drive. He went straight to the telephone and called the commandant at Stalag IID.

"These insolent Canadians refuse to work because they claim their living quarters are dirty. I insist you replace them with less demanding prisoners and severely discipline them when they return."

"You will give the Canadians whitewash and fresh straw," responded the commandant ignoring the owner's complaints. "They will clean the barracks and then they will work. Please put my sergeant on the telephone."

The Canadians received shovels, brooms, whitewash, brushes, and bales of straw. They spent the rest of the evening sprucing up their new quarters and relishing their victory over the Nazi.

"Tomorrow I'm catching a train to Stettin. The escape committee gave me the name of a contact and I have 500 cigarettes to pay for the crossing to Sweden. Before you know it, I'll be in England."

"Maurice, be careful. The Germans outside Stalag IID may not be as forgiving as those inside."

"Don't worry about me Jean-Pierre. I'll post you a letter from England."

The next day Maurice wore civilian clothes under his uniform and joined the work party. In the field, he laboured on the stumps near the stand of pine trees bordering the railway tracks. After removing two and depositing them in a pile, he moved towards some stumps closer to the line of trees. He waited for the guards to turn their backs then he slipped behind the trees. He held his breath waiting for the alarm to sound, but only heard the workers' picks and shovels and the guards talking. He worked his way through the woods towards the tracks and waited. He checked his watch. *Where's the bloody train?* After an anxious 15 minutes, a slow moving freight appeared. He waited for the locomotive to pass then bolted towards the tracks. He ran beside a boxcar with an open sliding door. He grabbed the door's handle and launched himself feet first into the opening. His lower body landed on the boxcar's dusty wooden floor with a thud. Only his grip on the door handle prevented him from falling backwards out of the car. With one hand on the handle and the other holding the edge of the door, he pulled himself into the boxcar. Exhausted, he lay on the floor for a few minutes. Once recovered, he removed all of his clothes, put his uniform back on, and the civilian clothes over it. Forty minutes later, the train slowed as it approached Stettin.

405-L-8707
(Records C)

1 March, 1944.

Mr. Michel Laekas,
1793 Beaudry,
Montreal, Quebec.

Dear Mr. Laekas:

Please be advised that official information has been received through the International Red Cross Committee, Geneva, Switzerland, that Stalag 8B, Germany, is now known as Stalag No. 344.

It is therefore necessary that all future letter mail and parcels be addressed accordingly.

You are further advised that any labels received from National War Services will bear the new Camp number Stalag No. 344.

Yours truly,

(C.L. Laurin) Colonel,
Director of Records,
for Adjutant-General.

ACR/EKG

Telegram from the Canadian Army notifying Jean-Pierre's father of Stalag VIIIB's name change. *Private Collection.*

DEPARTMENT OF NATIONAL DEFENCE
ARMY

CANADA

F.T.

OTTAWA, CANADA.

1 May 44

Mr. Michel Laekas,
1793 Beaudry,
Montreal, Quebec.

Re: D61894 L/Cpl. Jean Pierre LAEKAS,
Mont Royal Fusiliers (C.A.)

Dear Mr. Laekas:

Please be advised that information has been received through the Canadian Red Cross Society, London, England, that your son, who was previously being held a Prisoner of War at Stalag 344 has now been transferred to Camp Stalag 2D, Germany.

The Department of National War Services, who issue labels for next-of-kin parcels, have been notified of the above information for their necessary action.

Please rest assured that any further information received in this connection will be sent to you without delay.

Yours truly,

(C.L. Laurin) Colonel,
Director of Records,
for Adjutant-General.

NJM/ATG

30

Telegram from the Canadian Army notifying Jean-Pierre's father that he was transferred to Stalag IID. *Private Collection.*

Stalag IID - soccer field and guard tower. *Canadian War Museum, 19740246-013, Photo Archives T 1.10, Image #8.*

Stalag IID. 2 POWs, 1 civilian, 1 German officer. *Library and Archives Canada, Archival reference no. R778, File # 1 [3] e011052365.*

Fusiliers Gerard Landry (left), Jean-Pierre Laekas (middle), and Maurice Jolicoeur. Stalag IID. *Courtesy of Maurice Jolicoeur.*

Stalag IID. Maurice Jolicoeur and Jean-Pierre Laekas. *Courtesy of Maurice Jolicoeur.*

Chapter 29
Stargard, Germany - Stalag IID
Hope
June 1944–October 1944

On 6 June 1944, a small group of POWs gathered around one of the camps illicit radios to record the scheduled BBC broadcast.

"This is London. London calling in the home, overseas, and European Services of the BBC and through United Nations' radio Mediterranean. This is John Snagge speaking. Supreme Headquarters Allied Expeditionary Force have just issued communiqué number one and in a few seconds I will read it to you."

"What's the Allied Expeditionary Force?" asked one of the men.

"Be quiet. I want to hear what this is about," another exclaimed as he drew his ear closer to the radio.

"Allied naval forces supported by strong air forces began landing Allied armies this morning on the northern coast of France." After a pause the announcer continued, "I'll repeat that communiqué ...."

"Jesus Christ, they've invaded France."

The news spread like wildfire through the camp.

"What is going on? Why are you so happy?" asked a guard to a group of POWs.

"Haven't you heard? The Allies landed in northern France," announced a POW. "We'll be home by Christmas."

After several months at the farm, Arthur felt relaxed and comfortable in his new environment. The Nazi farm owner stayed

186

clear of the Canadians, no doubt remembering the guard's unveiled threat of reprisal. The farm's manager, a decent sort, assigned the men their work and ensured they had sufficient food, water, and rest to carry out their tasks. The 40 Canadians took pride in their work and in their spruced up living quarters. Although they were still prisoners, they created a family like atmosphere, which boosted their moral and provided them with a sense of freedom.

Of the two newly whitewashed buildings, the smaller building included a kitchen with an old enamel sink, a stove, and storeroom. A small latrine hut sat downwind and a respectable distance away from where they ate. Though the camp had no running water, the men could take the farm's horse-drawn tank wagon down to the village and fill it with water they pumped from the town's well. For bathing, the men heated water in a large copper behind the barracks. They worked from 0700 to 2000 hours with two and one-half hours allowed for meals. They did not want for food. In addition to the ample vegetables from the farm, they continued to receive Red Cross packages and parcels containing cigarettes.

Arthur made friends with a young German mother who worked in the fields alongside the Canadians. With his limited knowledge of German, he managed to converse with her. After receiving his share of a Red Cross parcel, he gave her some bars of chocolate for the children. The next day, she caught up with him during their lunch break.

"My children enjoyed the chocolate. I long for the day when we can put this war behind us and return to our normal lives. Last night, the radio announcer said the German armies resisted the Allies' attacks. The defeated armies' only hope is to retreat back across the Channel."

"You have a wireless?" blurted Arthur, not believing what he heard.

"Yes," she replied startled by Arthur's sudden outburst.

"May I borrow it?"

The women hesitated for a moment.

"I'll give you a package of cigarettes if you let me have it. I promise I'll return it to you."

That night in the barracks, the excited men talked about the radio.

"I can't wait to hear how the war's going. It can't last much longer," said a Fusilier.

The next day after dark, Arthur crept to an old work shed on the farm. The radio sat in a corner hidden by some farm tools. He wrapped the radio in his jacket then walked stealthily back to the barracks.

"I've got it," proclaimed Arthur as he entered.

"Bring it over here and I'll hook it up." Using electrical wire obtained from a guard in exchange for some cigarettes, a Fusilier jury-rigged the radio to the barracks' fuse box.

"Right, we're set," he said stepping back to give Arthur access.

The face of the worn, polished wooden box had two black knobs on either side of a small glass covered dial. Above the dial was a round opening covered by fabric. The men gathered around Arthur as he turned the black knob to switch on the radio. A steady hissing sound came from the speaker.

"Shit," said one of the anxious men.

"Be patient," responded Arthur as he slowly turned the dial. A German voice replaced the static. Arthur turned the dial and found another German station.

"I hope I didn't waste those cigarettes," said their electrician.

Arthur continued turning the knob until he found a station with music.

"You have been listening to the BBC Dancing Club with Victor Silvester and his Dance Orchestra."

Arthur waited to see what followed, hoping for a BBC news report. Another music program started. The men muttered and Arthur turned the dial to another station. A band played music and a commentator spoke, describing the scene at the crowded dance hall and the antics of the men and women dancing. Arthur turned the dial until he reached the end then he reversed through the stations. Only music played on the few English stations.

"Don't these fucking people know there's a war on?" yelled the electrician. "Listen to them. Those bastards have forgotten all about us."

A POW, devastated by the electrician's words, began to sob.

"Jesus Christ Arthur. Shut that damn thing off and get it out of here."

The summer passed with no news from Maurice. Jean-Pierre took this as a sign that his friend finally made it back to England. As autumn approached, positive news of the war from the camp's radios boosted the Canadians' morale. The Allies had advanced into Germany. On 21 October, Aachen, revered by Hitler as the home of Germany's First Reich, had the distinction of being the first German city captured. The Germans fought fiercely to defend their prized city but after a 20-day battle, they surrendered to U.S. forces. Although Jean-Pierre occupied his time with sports and translation activities, the Allies' progress left him impatient for an end to his captivity and a return to Mary. *My son is almost two years old. Is he calling someone else Daddy?* The unknown preyed on his mind. He read and reread Mary's letters hoping her words would somehow drive away his doubts.

Chapter 30
Stargard, Germany - Stalag IID
The Third Christmas in Captivity
November 1944–December 1944

Jean-Pierre walked briskly around the compound. The November wind cut through his uniform leaving his body chilled. Determined to get his exercise, he decided to do one more lap before heading back to the barracks. As he turned the last corner, he noticed a POW under guard entering the compound. *Who is it this time?* he wondered. Shivering, he picked up his pace.

"Jesus Christ!" He suddenly stopped. "Maurice? What have they done to you?" he said looking at his friend's sallow complexion, drawn face, and loosely hanging clothes.

"I'm fine, Jean-Pierre. Don't worry about me. Let's find a quiet corner and I'll tell you all about it."

They entered the barracks and sat at a vacant table.

"So what happened?"

"I almost made it," sighed Maurice. "I took the train to Stettin and got off before it reached the port. I found the harbour area and my contact."

"Where?"

"In a small café just off the main road. I told the guy I'd escaped from IID and wanted to get to Sweden. He said it would cost 1,000 cigarettes. I told him I only had the 500 the committee gave me before I left. I guess he felt sorry for me so he took the cigarettes."

Maurice paused and looked around the barracks. "I really didn't expect to be back here."

"Maurice, the war is coming to an end. Forget about these damn escapes. So what happened?"

"Early the next day, he took me and some other escapees to the commercial side of the port. We boarded a small, weather-beaten fishing boat. We hid below deck as best we could."

"Who were the other guys?"

"Four from Stalag IIA, two from XIA and a young RAF fighter pilot from Luft IV. We took off and were probably 40 miles out in the Baltic when a bloody German patrol boat stopped us. They searched the boat, found us, and shot the RAF pilot when he started screaming he wasn't going back."

"Did they kill him?"

"Must have. The bullets knocked the kid over the side and into the water. They didn't bother looking for him. They took us back to Stettin for questioning and I guess they found out about my other escapes. They weren't too happy with me. They put me in a salt mine and kept me there for months. Never saw the sun the whole time."

"Listen to me. Don't pull anymore of this shit. A few weeks ago, a guy from the Black Watch got killed trying to escape from here."

"Christ! What was his name?"

"Gerald Johnston. Apparently they shot him because he wouldn't raise his hands after they captured him."

"Bastards."

"Maurice, I'm telling you you'd better be careful."

A few weeks after Maurice's return, a distant rumble interrupted the POWs mid-day walk.

"Look over there," said Maurice pointing in the distance.

Hundreds of planes dotted the sky.

"They're attacking Stettin," exclaimed Jean-Pierre.

The force of the bombs' explosions shook the ground and rattled the barracks, shattering some windows. Though delighted by the sight of Allied bombers bringing the war to the Germans, the POWs refrained from cheering for fear of reprisals by the guards also watching the display.

As another Christmas approached, the anxious men listened to transcripts from the nightly BBC broadcasts. Sergeant Major Liscombe tracked the advancing Allied and Russian armies on escape maps and calculated the Russians to be less than 600 miles from Stargard.

"We'll be home by Christmas," said the ever-optimistic POW.

"This time you might not be far off your prediction," said his friend.

On 17 December, the men listened as their barracks' reporter read from his notes.

"Yesterday, the Germans launched a massive offensive against U.S. forces in the Ardennes region of Belgium. The attack included artillery barrages followed by armoured vehicles and thousands of troops."

"What the hell is going on?" asked a POW near the back of the group. "I thought the buggers were on the run."

"According to Eisenhower," continued the reporter, "in launching this offensive, the Germans have shortened the war for us. They've come out of their prepared defensive positions and though they may have achieved some initial success, they have shot their bolt."

As predicted, Germany's short-lived offensive faltered and became a fighting retreat as they gradually gave up all their newly won territory.

On Christmas Eve after hymn sing, Jean-Pierre joined Padre Foote's sermon. With food supplies in the camp deteriorating and the men's anxiety growing in terms of their salvation, the Padre called for the men to keep faith in themselves and the Lord. Jean-Pierre listened to Foote's words and cast his mind back to all that had happened. *I met a girl I loved. She gave me a son. I survived the massacre on the beach and continue to survive as a POW, in spite of the damn Krauts.* He did have faith in himself, but he believed more than ever, it was God who guided his destiny and who continually looked after him. He left the service buoyed by these thoughts. Later in the barracks, as he celebrated Réveillon with his Fusilier friends and comrades, he said a silent prayer.

Please Lord, make my third Christmas as a POW my last. Then he turned his thoughts to Mary and his son, trying to visualise their Christmas morning in Brighton.

Chapter 31
The Death March - Germany
January 1945–April 1945

The delivery of Red Cross packages dwindled to a trickle as the Allies advanced into Germany and the bombing of Germany's railroads continued unabated. The German military faced a bleak situation. From the west, the Allies advanced across a front stretching from the North Sea through part of the Netherlands, most of Belgium and all of France to the Mediterranean Sea. They also approached from the south having advanced up most of Italy's boot. From the east, the Russians and their Allies controlled a line through Eastern Europe from the Baltic Sea to the Adriatic Sea. By mid-January, Russian troops captured Warsaw, only 300 miles from Stargard. Rumours in the camp ran rampant as the POWs pondered their fate.

"I doubt the Germans are going to sit here and wait for the Russians," said an Aussie POW as he ate his meagre supper rations.

"I heard some guys saying the Germans may be planning to hold all POWs as hostages to negotiate some sort of deal with the Allies," said another POW.

"Hostages?" said Jean-Pierre with a worried look on his face. He continued eating his slice of black bread. *I'm not going to be a damn hostage for the bloody Germans.*

"Yeah, but they've got to move us out, because the Russians will reach us before our guys get here. The Russkis will come in with guns blazing and I doubt the risk of accidentally killing POWs in the process will stop them," replied the Aussie.

The next morning, Jean-Pierre and Maurice met up in the compound for their regular exercise routine. A biting wind cut into their exposed flesh making the -10C temperature even colder. The pale sun's tepid rays did little to warm them. Their boots crunched in the snow as they spoke of the rumours circulating in the camp.

"Do you think the Germans will keep us as hostages?"

"It's difficult to say but thank God we're not Russian," replied Maurice blowing warm air into his cupped hands. "Listen!" He suddenly stopped and cocked his head.

"What?"

"Can't you hear it? A popping sound followed by a rumbling."

"I can't hear a thing. Ever since Dieppe, I've had difficulty hearing."

"That's artillery and it's probably Russian."

"If it is, then I suspect it won't be long before we find out the Germans' plans."

Soon clusters of excited POWs stood outside the barracks stamping their feet and clasping their hands for warmth. They speculated on the source and reason behind the cannon fire. The barrage continued for over an hour and then stopped abruptly. The next day from the same direction came the faint sound of sporadic machine gun and rifle fire.

The German commandant conferred with his superiors then advised his officers to prepare for evacuation. Reports of massacres of German civilians and soldiers as the Russians swarmed like locusts over German occupied East Prussia weighed heavily in his decision. He doubted they would be any less vengeful when they arrived at Stalag IID.

On the morning of 2 February 1945, Sergeant Major Liscombe briefed them.

"This is it, boys. We're leaving."

The men cheered wildly until the sergeant major signalled for quiet.

"We're heading west for another camp. It's no surprise our guards don't want to wait for the Russians. They won't tell us where we're headed, perhaps because they don't know. However, they'll allow us to empty the stores of provisions. Be careful with the food since they don't know how long we'll be marching."

"Jesus Christ!" swore a Fusilier. "How the hell do they expect us to walk in this fucking blizzard?"

"Soldier, the correct form of address is Jesus Christ, Sergeant Major." The men chuckled at his witty reprimand.

"This is serious and your lives may depend on what I'm going to tell you, so listen up."

The humour of the situation vanished and the men quieted down.

"This is the coldest winter we've ever experienced. So scrounge whatever you can to keep warm." He pointed to the blankets, curtains, and articles of clothing hanging around the barracks. "I doubt there are sufficient accommodations along the way to house all of us. I'm also not sure how friendly the villagers will be. Don't forget, our Air Force has been bombing the shit out of their homes leaving some of them worse off than us. Stay together and don't try to escape. The Germans told us they will shoot anyone wandering away from the main column. If the Germans don't get you, there are all sorts of pissed off civilians out there who would love to get their hands on the enemy."

Several men frowned and looked at their friends perhaps rethinking their opportunities for escape.

"We're going to get through this but it will be tough. So, stay together, look out for your buddies, don't give up, and pray a lot."

In anticipation of another cold winter at the camp, Jean-Pierre had acquired from a German guard a pair of trousers, some gloves, and a pullover in exchange for cigarettes. Before leaving the camp, he pulled the extra trousers over his uniform without difficulty having lost so much weight. He put a spare pair of socks under his khaki shirt to keep them warm and dry, pulled the sweater on over his shirt, and then put on his battledress blouse. He tore a strip off his thin blanket, tied it around his ears, and then pulled on a knit cap. He put on his gloves, picked up his pack, and walked to the barracks door. He turned, took one last look at his home for the past year, and walked out into the blowing wind. He joined his formation standing in calf-high snow on the parade ground. They waited for instructions. As he inhaled, he felt the hair in his nostrils stick together. His warm breath swirled about his face in a mist as he exhaled.

The Germans evacuated the camp compound by compound and set the groups off on different routes to minimise congestion on the roads. To transport what they could not carry on their backs, some POWs used carts, wagons, and sleighs made of wood from their bunks. The horse-drawn and in some cases POW-drawn carts carried the Germans' supplies and those POWs unable to walk. Not wanting to get bogged down pulling anything, Jean-Pierre decided to carry all he could on his back. Trudging through snowdrifts, he joined the ragged column of POWs from his compound. They marched towards Stettin in the freezing weather for hours with little rest. As evening approached, Maurice, in a separate column, made out the skyline of Stettin in the distance. He shook his head as the memories of his last escape attempt played in his mind.

The Germans established a routine for the march, 15-20 miles each day for three days followed by one day of rest. As the men felt the effects of the march's pace, they discarded bulky and non-essential items they brought from camp. They knew they had to keep up with their column or risk death by either the guards or being alone in the bitter winter weather.

At night, Jean-Pierre joined other men in a search for shelter. Sometimes a deserted factory provided them protection from the elements. Other times a village church opened its doors to the men. For a few nights, they found refuge in barns where they slept in animal stalls, lying close together for warmth with a thin layer of foul smelling straw as their blanket. However, many nights, they spent the long, frigid hours in open fields, huddled together to stay warm. The morning after a night outside, Jean-Pierre faced excruciating pain, as he struggled to use muscles stiffened by the cold.

Early on, Jean-Pierre realised this journey would be the most severe test of all since that fateful day on the beach at Dieppe. Bitterly cold temperature and illness took a toll on the weak. Men fell by the wayside, either too exhausted or too ill to continue. The sick required hospitalisation to treat typhus, pellagra, pneumonia, or diphtheria brought on by the conditions. There were no hospitals and their companions could provide only basic medical care. Initially Jean-Pierre tried to help those who faltered, but soon realised he could do little to save them. Unable to maintain the pace, these men died from either a German's bullet or a slow, lonely death in the harsh winter weather. The march became a daily challenge to keep going.

The size of their column grew as they met up with German civilians fleeing the Russians, though the German guards ensured the civilians maintained their distance from the POWs. In some villages, sympathetic inhabitants gave the POWs food, handing it to them as the men walked by. The men treasured whatever they received, loaves of bread, fresh eggs, or fresh milk, water. In others villages, angry townsfolk lined the road to stone or spit at the men, blaming them for the misfortune war brought upon them and their community.

On 12 February, a report received at the International Red Cross headquarters in Geneva indicated occupants of Stalag IID were moving west to the other side of the Oder River. The report stated the formation included 1,112 Canadians. Remarkably, the Red Cross eventually found the POWs and distributed the life saving food packages. Although they had to share the package contents with more men than usual, Jean-Pierre relished every morsel he received. The Red Cross parcels provided only temporary relief from his hunger pains. Always on the lookout for food, at one farm he found the farmer's cache of root vegetables. The POWs stuffed their pockets and that night enjoyed a hot broth with their piece of black bread.

After weeks of keeping to the country roads, the German guards led the column to a paved two-lane divided highway. In the distance, Jean-Pierre saw a procession of horse-drawn carts headed in their direction.

"What the hell is that?" asked the POW walking beside him.

"They look like German soldiers."

As the two groups drew closer, Jean-Pierre realised the wagon-mounted force consisted of grim-faced youths and older men in German uniforms, some with weapons, and some without.

"In each wagon, there's a German who looks like a regular soldier. I bet he's there to make sure no one leaves," observed Jean-Pierre's companion.

"The Germans must be desperate if they think that lot stands a chance in battle," remarked Jean-Pierre surveying the wagons as they passed.

With his provisions from the camp gone, Jean-Pierre searched for food whenever they stopped. The Germans' starvation rations did little to maintain his strength. Any stray dog or cat venturing within reach risked becoming the evening's meal. When the carthorses faltered pulling the heavy loads because they too suffered from lack of food and water, the Germans shot them. Jean-Pierre enjoyed horsemeat while it lasted.

One day they approached a bridge spanning a wide river.

"Where are we?" asked the weary POW beside Jean-Pierre.

"I heard a guard just say this is the Elbe River."

"Christ. Isn't the Elbe River near the North Sea?"

"Yeah but it also runs right down through the middle of Germany. I don't even think the Germans know where we are."

Suddenly, the guards began yelling and gesturing for the POWs to leave the road. Jean-Pierre heard the drone of aircraft engines. He looked up. A flight of British Spitfires passed overhead and circled back, bearing down on the column.

"Shit! They think we're Germans," yelled Jean-Pierre.

The POWs ran for cover as quickly as their tortured limbs allowed. Jean-Pierre threw himself over a railing and tumbled down an embankment. He heard a high-pitched whistle as the aircraft dove towards the column of scattering men. Men still on the road frantically sought shelter, but for some it was too late as the planes' bullets tore through their bodies. Suddenly all was quiet except for the screams of the wounded and dying. Perhaps because they realised their error, the aircraft did not return to strafe the column again. Apart from some minor scratches and cuts, Jean-Pierre survived the ordeal, but 60 less fortunate POWs did not. With the help of the Germans, they buried their dead comrades in shallow graves alongside the road dug with pots, cups, and their bare hands.

Arthur and the 39 other Canadian POWs left the farm in the early morning of 1 January, one month before the evacuation of Stalag IID. They made a sleigh and put all their personal possessions on it. They emptied the kitchen of their farm vegetables placing them in their haversacks. With snow up to their knees, they marched for days under guard taking turns pulling the sleigh. Eventually other columns of POWs from nearby camps joined them.

Realizing conditions would only get worse, Arthur decided to escape. One night, as the guards took turns sleeping, Arthur and two friends managed to slip away unnoticed into the woods. Carrying only their haversacks, they travelled through the forest until they reached a road.

"Berlin is close by to the east," said Arthur reading the road sign.

"At least we have a rough idea where we are," said one of his travelling companions.

"Yeah, but we don't want to go to Berlin. Let's cross over and keep moving."

The three men crossed the Berlin autobahn twice more before they found a farm. They crouched in the woods looking for any activity from the house or German patrols. The farm appeared deserted. They quickly crossed the snow-covered field to the barn.

"Go see what you can find in the house while I hook up these horses," said Arthur's friend.

"Do you know what you're doing?"

"I was raised on a farm. I can do this with my eyes closed."

The two men took what little food they could find in the house. When they returned to the barn, the horses stood in their harnesses ready to pull the wagon.

"Come on. Get up here before somebody spoils all this."

They travelled along country roads during the day and slept in the cart at night. Near a small village, they ran into a patrol of Russian soldiers. The Russians pointed their weapons at the men, but did not shoot. They gestured for the three POWs to get down from the cart.

"Tovarich," said Arthur using the Russian word for comrade he picked up at Stalag IID.

A Russian officer approached. He held a large black pistol in his hand.

"Tovarich?" questioned the officer casually pointing the pistol first at himself and then Arthur.

"Da," replied Arthur nodding his head enthusiastically as he reached for his identification tag hanging from his neck.

His sudden movement startled the Russian soldiers who quickly brought their weapons to bear on Arthur. The officer calmed them and advanced to inspect the tag. The man's pungent breath filled Arthur's nostrils.

"Tovarich," said the officer nodding his head as he displayed the tag for his men.

Arthur relaxed and smiled as the Russian shook his hand. The officer noticed the watch on Arthur's wrist. He grinned broadly, rolled up his sleeve, and proudly displayed a variety of watches.

"Germans kaput," said the Russian grinning. He touched the watches and then drew his finger across his throat signifying the fate of the owners.

A Russian soldier called out, interrupting their exchange. He pointed up the road. A German truck with soldiers in the back approached. A German soldier stood on the running board holding on to the cab with one hand. In his other hand, he waved a white flag high above his head. The Russian officer barked a command. Arthur jumped, startled by the sound of gunfire as the Russians raked the truck with bullets. When the shooting stopped, the Russian soldiers finished off survivors with a single shot to their head. The officer surveyed the scene, touched the watch on his wrist, pointed to the lifeless bodies beside the motionless truck, and gestured for Arthur to join him.

The attack by the British planes on the column left Jean-Pierre numb. It took all his willpower to keep going. He could not keep track of how long they marched as one day melded with another. He tried to judge where they were heading by the sun. First, they travelled west, then south, then north, then south again. He was too weak and too cold to care anymore. He struggled to put one foot in front of the other. He tightened his belt to the last notch but still his trousers gradually slipped to his hips and would have made their way down to his knees if he did not occasionally hike them back up. They stumbled along like emotionless, stiff-legged zombies. When they stopped for a rest, Jean-Pierre sat on his backpack to relieve the pain when the bones in his behind encountered the hard ground. Weeks passed without any sign of the Red Cross and their lifesaving parcels. With their supplies gone, Jean-Pierre ate grass, shrubs, and roots, to help subdue the gnawing hunger pangs.

His spirits received a much-needed boost as the winter receded and the longer, brighter days of spring arrived. He felt the warmth of the sun on his back and walking became easier once the snow disappeared. *I'm going to make it.* His homecoming appeared like a mirage before him giving him strength. *Mary and Michael John will be waiting for me. I'll kiss them both. We'll walk together along the promenade in Brighton. The sun will be out and a gentle sea breeze will be coming in off the water. I'll get a job and buy a little house by the sea, somewhere quiet. Mary will stay home and take care of Michael John. I'll be at peace with mankind and everything will be right in our little world.*

On 5 April, the Germans confidently led the weak and hungry column of POWs along a busy road. In the distance through the trees, Jean-Pierre saw guard towers standing high above a barbed wire fence. *As desperate as I am to get home, right now I'll settle for another damn POW camp. As long as I don't have to march anymore.*

Chapter 32
Fallingbostel, Germany
Stalag XIB
April 1945

After marching almost 700 miles in two months, Jean-Pierre and the haggard columns of POWs staggered into Stalag XIB at Fallingbostel, Germany. Curious inmates in nearby compounds watched the line of emaciated men wearily make their way to the parade ground. Once assembled and counted, the Germans took the men to the delousing centre to rid them of the lice infesting their bodies and clothing. Jean-Pierre had not taken his clothes off or washed since leaving Stalag IID on 2 February.

"We're not going to be here much longer," said a POW working at the delousing centre.

"What do you mean?" asked Jean-Pierre.

"One of the guards told me we're moving north of the Elbe."

At the camp kitchen, Jean-Pierre received a cup of watery grass and cabbage soup with a small portion of black bread made from rye, sugar beets, leaves, and sawdust. He welcomed the meagre servings though it did little to relieve his hunger. After his meal, the guards took the POWs to some deserted barracks. Jean-Pierre ignored the filthy state of the interior. He headed straight for an empty bunk on the bottom tier, knowing he did not have the strength to climb to the upper bunks. He dropped his haversack on the floor then collapsed on the straw mattress. He lay there unable to move, his body numb from months of abuse. He could not have lasted much longer; his weakened body would have eventually given in to the hunger, dysentery, or pneumonia that claimed many of his comrades. He shook his head trying to block out the images of his friends who either fell by the wayside or died during their sleep. *I don't care what they do to me. I'm not going on another march. Either I'll leave this camp as a free man or I'll die here.* Exhausted, he closed his eyes and slept soundly for the first time in months.

The next day, he joined the other new arrivals assembling on the parade ground for a briefing about camp conditions.

"There isn't much good news," said the resident sergeant major. "Daily rations are down to one loaf of bed board bread between 10 of you. You'll get half a pint of soup to wash it down, and I use the term soup very loosely to describe the concoction. There is no running water. The latrines are full and they aren't being emptied. We haven't received parcels from the Red Cross since I can't remember when, and the camp's reserve of parcels has long since been depleted." He paused for a moment but no one spoke. The men stared straight ahead, not believing what they heard.

"There is good news," said the sergeant major. "The Russians have crossed the Oder, and the Brits and Yanks are closing in from the other side. I hope they'll get here soon but it looks like the Krauts don't plan to give up. They've got tanks and soldiers dug in nearby on the Lüneburg Heath."

"I hope those fuckers get blown to hell," muttered the POW standing ahead of Jean-Pierre.

"We'll settle our accounts with these bastards later," responded the sergeant major. "Be ready to take shelter once the shelling starts. Leave the fighting to our guys. Don't do anything stupid or brave. I don't want to bury any of you here."

After the briefing, Jean-Pierre walked back to his hut. *Despite the filth and lack of food, at least we've stopped the endless walking.* He heard someone call his name, interrupting his thoughts. He turned to see Maurice with a huge grin on his face sauntering towards him. The two hugged each other and laughed, each relieved the other had survived.

"They're planning to move us again, somewhere beyond the Elbe River," said Jean-Pierre.

"What?"

"A Brit working at the delousing centre told me."

"There can't be much German territory left that's not being threatened by the Allies and Russians."

"Maybe not but I also heard they marched 12,000 Brits out of the camp a few weeks ago. No one knows where they were headed."

"Christ, when are our guys going to get here?"

"Maurice, I'm telling you now. I'm not going on another march."

Long before Jean-Pierre's arrival, the once tolerable conditions at Stalag XIB began to deteriorate due to constant overcrowding. In February 1945, the International Red Cross inspected the camp and issued a report criticizing the camp conditions. "...*and we are greatly disturbed at the appalling conditions at this once excellent camp. There is almost an entire lack of sanitary arrangements, fuel, blankets, sleeping accommodations, medical facilities, and materials. The conditions show a gross disregard of the principles of the Geneva Convention....*"

A week passed and Jean-Pierre doubted his chances for survival. His hunger pains grew and the sounds of coughing, wheezing, spitting, and moaning surrounded him. Each morning, a wagon carried those who died during the night to the graveyard for burial. *Please God, don't let me end up in that damn wagon.*

Jean-Pierre woke to the sharp crack of cannons followed by explosions as shells landed close to his barracks. POWs scattered everywhere looking for shelter. Jean-Pierre found a trench and tumbled in beside another Fusilier.

"This is it," shouted Jean-Pierre. "This has to be our guys." A salvo of shells exploded nearby sending dirt and rubble into their trench.

"Jesus Christ," cried the Fusilier beside him. "We're going to die."

Please God, not now. Don't let me die now, prayed Jean-Pierre. *The war is almost over.* He pressed his body against the damp earth and put his arms over his head trying to block out the sounds of battle.

Sporadic shelling continued through the day. Jean-Pierre remained crouched in the trench as the unseen combatants fought in the rolling hills, fields, and woods of the heathland. As the sun began to set, the shelling stopped and a nervous quiet descended on the camp. The men crept cautiously out of their shelters and congregated in the compound.

"I wonder where they are," commented an American POW as he peered down the camp road.

"They probably packed it in for the night," joked a Fusilier. "If they're Brits, they've got to have their tea."

On 16 April, two Chaffee reconnaissance tanks of the 8th Kings Royal Irish Hussars rumbled up the road and ground to a halt outside the camp's gates.

"Christ," said the driver of the lead vehicle. Dirty, skeletal figures with drawn faces and sunken eyes peered through the fence. "They look as bad as the inmates at Bergen-Belsen. Who are they?"

Realizing the tanks were British, the POWs cheered wildly. The German guards recognised they had no other option but to open the gates. The POWs surrounded their British liberators as they entered the camp. Shocked at the sight of the starving prisoners, the Hussars offered them their water, rations, and cigarettes. Maurice noticed one of his tormentors from the march without his rifle and moved towards the German, seeking to repay in kind the brutality the guard had inflicted on the POWs.

"Sorry mate," said a burly tank crewman as he restrained Maurice. "As much as I understand and would like to see the bastards suffer just like they made you suffer, I've got orders to make sure there are no reprisals."

Within hours, additional British soldiers arrived, bringing military rations, bread, and real tea. Doctors and medics attended to the men. They cautioned the newly liberated POWs to eat small portions since too much food ingested too quickly might kill them. Nearby a British officer stood on a jeep and addressed the thousands of men in the compound.

"Gentlemen, as soon as transportation can be arranged, you'll be taken to a transit camp in Belgium. From there you'll be flown back to England."

POWs cheered, laughed, and some cried uncontrollably.

"It'll take a few days, so in the meantime, we'll be looking after you here at the camp. With your help, we'll tidy things up and make you as comfortable as possible in this god-forsaken place. You're free to come and go as you please, but don't leave this area. Don't drink the water in the streams, it's polluted. And stay away from the Russian compound. It's full of disease."

Maurice and some friends walked to a nearby village and returned with a cow they stole from an angry but outnumbered farmer. Despite the warning about consuming too much food, Maurice and Jean-Pierre enjoyed the best tasting steak they had ever eaten.

That evening, Jean-Pierre stretched out on his bunk with his hands cushioning his head. *Is it a dream? Will I wake up and find myself still a prisoner? Are my years of torment really over?* He savoured the moment, smiled, and closed his eyes. *No, it's not a dream. I'm finally free. I'm going home to Mary and my son.*

The day after their liberation, a British soldier gave Jean-Pierre a bar of soap, a razor, a mirror, and a bowl of steaming water. He found a convenient location inside the barracks and propped the mirror up on a window ledge.

"Jesus Christ!" He stood motionless in front of the mirror. Dark, sunken eyes in a drawn, emaciated face stared back at him. He gaped in disbelief at his reflection. A grim mask replaced his youthful features. He touched his forehead and ran his fingers down the tight, sallow skin stretching over his cheekbones. Tears formed in his eyes. *Mary will never recognise me. I can't go back looking like this.* He splashed the hot water on his bearded face and rubbed it vigorously with soap hoping to transform himself into the man he once was. He calmed himself and looked once again in to the mirror. *Those bastards did this to me but I'll get back in shape. I know I can.*

He put together a simple regime to restore his body. He ate small but frequent portions of simple food his stomach would tolerate and slowly exercised around the compound until he needed to rest.

After almost three weeks in Stalag XIB, Jean-Pierre wondered if the Canadian army had forgotten about them. In spite of the appalling conditions at the camp, the British liberators did everything they could to make the men comfortable. They gave them free rein to leave the camp but most of the death march survivors including Jean-Pierre could only manage to walk around the compound.

Death march route from Stalag IID to Stalag XIB. *Private Collection.*

Stalag XIB, Fallingbostel, Germany. *Courtesy of*
http://www.fallingbostelmilitarymuseum.de/stalag/stalag.htm

Stalag XIB, Fallingbostel, Germany. *Courtesy of*
http://www.fallingbostelmilitarymuseum.de/stalag/stalag.htm

Stalag XIB, Fallingbostel, Germany. *Courtesy of*
http://www.fallingbostelmilitarymuseum.de/stalag/stalag.htm

Stalag XIB, Fallingbostel, Germany. *Courtesy of*
http://www.fallingbostelmilitarymuseum.de/stalag/stalag.htm

Chapter 33
Brussels, Belgium
Free at Last
April 1945–May 1945

"They're here," yelled a Fusilier rushing into the barracks. Jean-Pierre raced to the door. A convoy of British army trucks covered by tan canvas were entering the camp gates and parking side-by-side in the main compound. Jean-Pierre was ready. He returned to his bunk and picked up the haversack containing all his personal belongings. Without waiting for his sergeant major to call the men to assemble, he left the barracks and headed for the parked vehicles.

The British transported the Canadians to a captured German airfield where a fleet of olive-drab aircraft waited for them.

"End of the line, gentlemen," called an officer approaching Jean-Pierre's truck as the tailgate slammed down. "That's your plane over there."

Jean-Pierre looked in the direction the officer pointed. The large two-engine aircraft sat in a reclining position with its nose snobbishly high in the air and its tail held just above the ground by a small wheel. Seven square windows above the wing ran from the plane's front to its back, stopping before a large opening near the tail. A soldier standing inside the opening motioned them forward.

"She's carried everything from paratroopers to toilet paper and she'll get you to Brussels, no problem," continued the officer trying to reassure the men.

Jean-Pierre eased himself down from the truck and joined the queue leading to the aircraft. *This can't be any worse than the S.S. Antonia,* he thought. *There's a first time for everything just as long as it gets me the hell out of here.* When he reached the plane, he put his foot on the bottom rung of the metal fold-down ladder. As the man ahead of him disappeared into the plane, Jean-Pierre stepped up awkwardly to the top rung. The soldier standing at the entrance took Jean-Pierre's arm and pulled him into the plane.

"Make your way forward."

Jean-Pierre walked between the occupied metal seats lining each side of the fuselage. He sat on the floor next to another Fusilier. From the front of the plane, a young man appeared. He wore an RAF uniform and held a pipe between his teeth as he surveyed the scene.

"I need you chaps sitting on the floor to move towards the rear of the plane. This'll help us get airborne sooner and enable us to make it over the trees just past the end of the runway."

Jean-Pierre looked at the pilot in disbelief.

"Don't fret mate," he said seeing Jean-Pierre's concerned look. "I've done this hundreds of times. The odds are in our favour."

After the men shuffled towards the back, the pilot gave them the thumbs up sign and returned to the cockpit.

"I don't think he understands the priori theory of probability," said the Fusilier seated on the floor beside Jean-Pierre.

"What are you talking about?" asked Jean-Pierre.

"His chances of making it get worse, not better, the more often he does it."

"Christ, don't tell me that. I haven't survived 32 months as a POW to end up dead in a plane crash."

A high-pitched whine echoed through the cabin followed by a rumble as one of the engines came to life. Once it was running smoothly, the other engine started. A short while later, the plane taxied across the rough ground, jolting the passengers sitting on the hard metal floor. Jean-Pierre slid his haversack beneath him providing a cushion for his tailbone. The aircraft turned onto the runway then came to an abrupt stop.

"This is it," said the odds maker.

The engines' pitch increased until their roar drowned out the men's nervous small talk. The aircraft moved slowly as the engines strained to overcome the inertia of the heavily laden plane. Jean-Pierre hunched his shoulders forward and lowered his head in a protective position. The plane's bumping motion increased as it raced forward. Jean-Pierre closed his eyes, visualising the line of tall trees approaching. Suddenly, the constant vibration beneath him stopped. He felt a roller coaster sensation in his stomach. The force of the acceleration pushed the soldiers sitting on the floor backwards into the knees of the soldiers behind them.

"Christ," muttered Jean-Pierre. "What a way to travel."

The plane soared into the air, just clearing the treetops.

"Shit, that was close," said a Fusilier at a window seat.

Jean-Pierre tried to get comfortable on the crowded floor. He looped his right arm around the floor support of the seat next to him then leaned against the seat. He somehow managed to sleep, lulled by the constant drone of the plane's engines. He woke hours later as the plane banked in a steep turn.

"I can see an airfield," shouted the Fusilier with the window seat.

Jean-Pierre felt the plane level out. The roller coaster sensation in his stomach returned as the plane descended. Minutes later, the plane's wheels slammed down on the steel matting covering the airfield's grass runway. The aircraft's right tire burst from the force of the impact. The men on the floor cursed as they pitched forward into the backs of the men in front of them. The plane travelled a short distance before the drag on the right wheel collapsed the landing gear. The right wing tip dug in and threw the plane into a vicious ground loop. Jean-Pierre crashed against the metal seats beside him. The aircraft gave a final lurch and came to rest. A crew member kicked the cargo door open and yelled for the men to get out. Jean-Pierre struggled to his feet. He hurriedly made his way to the exit not knowing what else to expect and jumped to the ground. He walked away from the plane rubbing his right shoulder.

"Thank you," he said looking skyward.

Their plane landed at Gosselies south of Brussels. The Allies used the small airfield to support their advances in to Germany. The runway's steel matting enabled heavier military aircraft to land on the soft ground underneath. Unfortunately, a Fusilier sitting on the floor died during the landing. The force of the impact threw him against the fuselage, breaking his neck. The tragic death of their comrade dampened the Fusiliers' jubilant mood.

"What was the fucking point of him surviving all that we've been through just to die in a stupid, fucking plane crash?" asked the dead Fusilier's friend with tears rolling down his cheeks.

"His time had come, just as it will for all of us," comforted his friend.

"No. He didn't deserve that." He sobbed uncontrollably. "He didn't deserve to die."

During the truck ride to Brussels, Jean-Pierre pondered the dead Fusilier's fate and his own. *Was there a predetermined time for all of us? And if so, when's mine?* Two hours later, the trucks pulled in to Place Charles Rogier in downtown Brussels. Jean-Pierre felt weak and slightly nauseated, not having eaten since leaving Fallingbostel. His leg and back muscles had stiffened from the hours he sat on the truck's wooden bench. He accepted help from a couple of soldiers assisting the emaciated Canadians as they attempted to climb down. Once on solid ground, he held onto the side of the truck until he regained his strength. He looked around. He stood in a large open cobblestoned square surrounded by high stone buildings.

"Follow the line, soldier," called a Military policeman pointing towards a tall narrow building sandwiched between two shorter ones.

"What did you call me?" asked Jean-Pierre.

"Soldier," responded the MP in a gruff voice. "Is that a problem?"

"No," he said smiling. "I haven't been called a soldier in three years." He hoisted his haversack over his shoulder. *I'm still a Fusilier!*

He stood in line and looked up at the building facing him. A large sign identified it as the Cosmopolite. Beneath, another sign proclaimed THE MAPLE LEAF FOR CANADIANS. On a broad terrace above the entrance, the Canadian Red Ensign waved gently from a flagpole.

"We're staying in a bloody hotel," said the Fusilier in front of him. "Imagine that. We've gone from a Kraut camp to a hotel."

"Jean-Pierre entered the hotel struck by the leather chairs, mirrors, carpeted floors, and wood panelling that greeted him. *What a difference a day makes!* Canadian soldiers in the lobby stopped their conversations to watch the line of skinny men in their filthy battledress.

"Identification number," said the Canadian army clerk behind the counter.

"26652," replied Jean-Pierre. "Shit, what am I saying? I'm D61894, Laekas, Jean-Pierre. Les Fusiliers Mont-Royal."

"Follow the line to your left down the hall to the barbershop," said the clerk without looking up as he recorded the information in his register.

Jean-Pierre waited his turn until one of the barbers motioned for him to sit.

"Just a trim."

"Certainly sir," replied the barber covering him with an apron. In less than a minute, all his matted locks lay on the floor.

After joining another line headed to the showers, he removed his tattered clothes and worn boots depositing them in a bin. In the communal wash area, he lathered his body with soap and rubbed his bald head vigorously with the tips of his fingers, hoping to rid himself of any parasites. He lingered under the warm water, letting it flow down his face and body. He picked up a towel and smiled. *I haven't seen one of these in years.* He dried himself then lined up with other naked soldiers at the delousing centre.

"Close your eyes and mouth, put your hands above your head, and block your nose," said a man hidden behind a half-face respirator and goggles. In his gloved hands, he held a rod attached by a hose to a large drum.

Jean-Pierre did as instructed. He heard the compressor start and felt the tingling spray of some substance, starting at his head and moving down his body.

"Turn around." The delouser continued spraying.

"Okay, you're done. Don't bathe for 24 hours."

Jean-Pierre could taste the bitter powder on his lips. He followed the line to the next station. A Canadian army doctor performed a cursory physical examination.

"How do you feel? Any pains?"

"No sir."

"Step on the scales. What's your normal weight, son?"

"About 175 pounds sir."

The doctor slid the weight along the beam until the arrow hovered over a horizontal line.

"You're 105 right now. It's going to take quite a while before you gain what you've lost. We're going to feed you small portions because your system won't be able to handle too much food."

"Yes sir. I understand. That's what the doctor told me at XIB."

"Good man. Right then, off you go."

At the last station, he received a new uniform, 800 francs, and a Canadian issued map of the city. Later that night, Jean-Pierre relaxed in the small hotel room he shared with another Fusilier. He looked out the window and watched more trucks enter the lit square bearing weary, liberated POWs. *I can't believe just a few short hours ago that was me.* He felt reborn. He looked in the mirror and smiled at his reflection. There he stood with a clean body and a new uniform. *We're not there yet, but you look a thousand times better than the last time we met.*

"Arthur, where the hell have you been?" asked a Fusilier in the hotel lobby.

"The same place as you, washing away three years' worth of dirt, lice, and crap." He looked at his reflection in the lobby mirror. He enjoyed the feel of his new uniform.

"Christ Arthur. You didn't finish the march with us after we left the farm. We thought you were dead."

"It's a long story," he said adjusting the angle of his cap. "Let's have a beer, and I'll tell you all about it."

"You're on."

They left the hotel and turned down Rue Des Croissades. Three well-dressed, pretty, young women approached them.

"Hello soldiers. Can we show you a good time?" asked a girl with dark brown eyes and long brown hair. She spoke English with a strong French accent.

"How much?" asked Arthur in French getting straight to the business at hand.

"Eight hundred francs," replied the girl without hesitating. She smiled at the Canadians, happy they could speak French. She moistened her lips with the tip of her tongue.

"Ha!" scoffed Arthur shaking his head. "Peasant girls outside the fence at Stalag VIIIB performed a strip tease for the price of a bar of soap." He chuckled at his riposte and pushed his way past the women. They cursed him in French and then turned their attention to a group of soldiers on the other side of the street.

In the bar over several glasses of beer, Arthur told his companion about his escape from the death march, the autobahn, and his encounter with the Russians.

"We travelled with the Russians for about three weeks. Some French POWs joined up with us, but the Russians made it clear they didn't like the Frenchmen. I don't know why they didn't but the Frenchmen soon set out on their own."

"But the Russkis didn't mind you?"

"No. We got on famously. They took us to a town full of Russian soldiers and gave us a room in a hotel. We rested for a few days and then left."

"Where did you go?"

"The Russians gave us directions to a nearby American base. We eventually found it. The Americans took us in and gave us breakfast. I can still see it," he said closing his eyes. "Two fresh eggs, sunny side up, bacon, toast, and real coffee. You know how long it had been since I had real bloody coffee?"

His friend nodded at Arthur's rhetorical question.

"Eighteenth of August, nineteen bloody forty-two," exclaimed Arthur. "After breakfast, a U.S. soldier drove us to the nearest town. We found a pastry shop and helped ourselves to some small cakes and tarts. This woman came out from the back room screaming for us to leave. We just yelled back at her with our mouths full and left. The soldier told us there was a large U.S. air base up the road, so we stole a motorcycle and drove to the airfield. Three days later, they flew us to Brussels. "

Jean-Pierre never used his 800 Belgian Francs and the map of Brussels identifying the city's various activities and sights. Like many others, he did not have the strength to trek around the city's labyrinth of streets and lanes. He met up with Maurice and together they passed the time reading, taking short walks, and talking about their experience.

On 30 April, Jean-Pierre returned to the hotel after a brief walk. The crowded lobby was full of cheering soldiers.

"The bastard is dead! The fucking bastard is dead!" shouted a soldier beside Jean-Pierre.

"Who's dead?"

The soldier gave Jean-Pierre a newspaper with bold headlines that announced the death of Adolf Hitler.

On 10 May 1945, Jean-Pierre boarded a B-24 Liberator for the flight to an RAF base in England. Throughout the flight, he thought about the chain of events that resulted in his capture at Dieppe. *What could I have done differently? I'm going back not as a proud soldier who fought the good fight, but as a former POW who sat on his ass while others fought and died.* The shame he felt when first captured slowly engulfed him. He dreaded returning to his regiment.

The Cosmopolite Hotel, requisitioned as the Maple Leaf leave centre for Canadian military personnel, Brussels, Belgium, 22 October 1944. *Lieut. Frank L. Dubervill / Library and Archives Canada / Dept. of National Defence / PA-116751*

CANADIAN FORCES

YOU

Are on leave in

Brussels

This map is presented to assist you in your visit to the City. A variety of information is given and for any details not shown visit the bureau.

Canadian
Hospitality and Information Bureau,
33, Boulevard du Régent.

Operated by
Canadian Knights of Columbus War Services
on behalf of
Canadian Legion War Services Inc.
Canadian Y. M. C. A. Overseas
Salvation Army Canadian War Services.

Leave map of Brussels, Belgium, WWII. *Canadian War Museum, Leave map of Brussels, Issue No. 4, scheme H [cartographic material], 19800548-056, Textual Records 58A 1 40.14.*

CANADIAN ACCOMMODATION CENTRES

CANADA CLUB : 32-33, Boulevard du Régent. Day Club for O. R.

and

Hospitality and Information Bureau. For all Ranks.

ATLANTA HOTEL : Boulevard Adolphe Max.

Hotel for Canadian Officers
Officer's snack-Bar. Dancing 5 to 11 p. m.

MAPLE LEAF HOTEL : Place Rogier.

Leave hotel for Cdn. O. R's. — Group of 7 hotels. — Meals served at Cosmopolite. — Snack-Bars and Canteens.

23, Avenue DE LA TOISON D'OR : Leave Hotel for Canadian O. R's. — Meals will be served at. Canada Club. — 32, Boulevard du Régent.

BLUE POOL : Swimming pool; bath, shower. 25, Rue St. François. For all Ranks.

35, Rue de la Loi : Canadian See H. Q. Brussels Garrison.

10-10a, Petite Rue du Nord : Canadian O. R. Leave Hotel.

CONCERTS

PALAIS DES BEAUX-ARTS : Rue Royale. Sunday 2.30 P. M.

THEATRES

ENSA

Théâtre Royal du Parc : Rue de la Loi.
Variety Theatre : Rue de Malines.
Scala Theatre : Place de Brouckère (Boulevard Adolphe Max) (Forces only).

OTHERS

Théâtre Royal de la Monnaie : Place de la Monnaie (Opera-Ballet).
Théâtre des Galeries Saint-Hubert : Galerie du Roi (Comedy-Vaudeville).
Théâtre de Vaudeville : Galerie de la Reine (Vaudeville).
Théâtre de l'Alhambra : Boulevard E. Jacqmain (Revues).
Théâtre Folies Bergère : Rue des Croisades (Flemish only).
Palais d'Eté : Rue Grétry (Music Hall).
Royal Circus : Rue de l'Enseignement.
ABC Theatre : Place de l'Yser.

CONCERTS

Royal Conservatory of Music : Rue de la Régence.
3PM Sunday and Thurs.
7PM other days.
Théâtre de la Monnaie : Place de la Monnaie. Sun. 2.30 PM.

Leave map of Brussels, Belgium, WWII. *Canadian War Museum, Leave map of Brussels, Issue No. 4, scheme H [cartographic material], 19800548-056, Textual Records 58A 1 40.14.*

Chapter 34
England
May 1945

Upon their arrival in England, British military trucks took Jean-Pierre and the other liberated POWs to Euston station on the outskirts of London. They had time to kill before boarding a troop train to Camp Aldershot where a lengthy repatriation process awaited them. British civilians at the station stared at the hundreds of gaunt men in Canadian Army uniforms. An elderly woman approached Jean-Pierre and took his hand.

"Thank you," she said and walked away.

The woman's simple act of appreciation left Jean-Pierre perplexed. He never thought of his ordeal as other than an adventure that had gone horribly wrong.

"What did she say to you?" asked Maurice as he joined his friend.

"She thanked me."

"For what?"

"That's exactly what I thought."

"Did I tell you about my ride from Brussels?" said Maurice changing the subject.

"You flew here, just like the rest of us."

"Not like the rest of you. Before the flight, I met the pilot of one of the B-24s. I told him my brother flies transports in the RAF."

"Did he know him?"

"He said he didn't. I guess there are a lot of pilots in the RAF. He offered to let me fly in the empty navigator's spot."

"Where's that?"

"Right up front in the nose," said Maurice with a broad grin. "Christ Jean-Pierre. I had a better view than the pilot did. It's all clear plastic up front, even the floor."

"So how was it?"

"Incredible. On take-off, that old runway just raced past me. While we were in the air, I could see everything."

"Did you take any photos?"

"Damn no. I didn't have my camera. It was amazing but the landing scared the hell out of me."

"Really? Nothing ever scares you, Maurice."

"Just imagine, perched in a little plastic bubble travelling over 100 miles an hour as the trees, houses, and buildings come rushing up at you. Shit, I almost passed out when we landed." He paused and looked around the station. "All this talking has made me thirsty. There's a pub over there. Let's go for a drink."

"You go Maurice. I don't think my stomach could take it."

Jean-Pierre relaxed on one of the benches near the tracks. He thought back to the woman who thanked him. *What would she have said if she knew I sat on my ass in a prison camp for three years while others did the fighting?*

"A glass of Laphroaig, straight up," said Maurice as he caught the barman's eye.

The man nodded and took an emerald green bottle with a broad white label from the shelf behind him. He poured a generous amount of the gold coloured liquid into a glass and put it on the counter.

"Thank you." He lifted the glass, tossed it back, and ordered another. The next thing he knew, he was boarding the train supported by two fellow Fusiliers.

"What happened?" asked Maurice.

"You passed out," replied one of the men laughing. "You downed the Scotch and then the Scotch downed you."

At the Aldershot train station, the soldiers boarded Canadian Military trucks that transported them to the No. 1 Canadian Reception Depot in the nearby village of Church Crookham. Jean-Pierre was relieved to see they were not going directly to the Fusiliers' base. Their stay at the Reception Depot was brief, just long enough for the clerk to transfer each name from the POW list to the hospital admission list. They once again boarded trucks, this time heading to the No. 4 Canadian General Hospital just outside of Aldershot. Jean-Pierre joined the admissions' queue winding its way down the corridor to the outside door. When his turn came, a clerk registered his name then sent him to a nurse seated at a nearby table. Over her blue uniform, the nurse wore a white, starched smock and on her head, a white headpiece with a train that trailed down to her shoulders. Jean-Pierre had never seen anything so clean and fresh looking as the young girl's apron.

"Please have a seat," said the nurse with a warm smile and gesturing to the chair beside the table.

"Are you a nun?"

"No, I'm a nursing sister. We're members of the Royal Canadian Army Medical Corps, but we're still called nursing sisters."

"You're part of the Canadian Army?"

"Yes, now I would like you to tell me about any aches and pains you have before I send you to see the doctor."

"I feel fine and I want to get released."

"Right then. The sooner you see the doctor, the sooner you'll be getting out of here. Let's get you ready." She made an entry on the register, stood up, and led Jean-Pierre to a room. A folded pair of pyjamas lay on the bed.

"Please remove your clothes, put on the pyjamas, and the doctor will see you shortly."

Jean-Pierre had dozed off when a doctor, carrying a clipboard in his hands, entered the room. Startled, he swung his legs over the side of the bed, ready to stand at attention.

"Don't bother getting up for me young man because I'm just going to ask you to lie down so I can examine you."

He began to methodically prod, poke, look, and listen to Jean-Pierre's body, occasionally asking him questions about his POW experiences. Once finished, he made a few notes in the file.

"It'll be a long, slow process before your body fully recovers from the malnutrition. This is not something we can rush. The nurse told me you're anxious to leave. You will eventually be discharged but not before I say you can. Is that clear?" said the doctor locking eyes with Jean-Pierre.

"Yes sir."

Though he longed to see Mary and his son, Jean-Pierre resigned himself for a stay in the hospital, partly because he knew the doctor was right, but also because it delayed his inevitable return to his regiment. His first week at the hospital consisted of eating nine small meals a day, light exercise, and a lot of reading. His dark hair had grown back since Brussels and he gradually put on some weight. The face in the mirror staring back at him each morning as he shaved began to lose its tired and drawn appearance. While convalescing, he spent many hours debating whether to return to his regiment once discharged from the hospital or to go straight to Brighton and risk being absent without leave. He felt his reception at the Regiment at best would be cool. After all, they would be more interested in the activities of real soldiers, not spectators like him who watched as the war went by. At least in Brighton, people would be glad to see him. His mind turned to his homecoming. *We're on our own, I kiss Mary passionately and hold her tight. Then I pick up Michael John in my arms and we walk along the promenade in Brighton with the gentle sea breeze caressing our faces.*

On 22 May, Lance Corporal Laekas received his hospital discharge. Instead of boarding the truck to take him back to the regiment, he hitched a ride to the Aldershot train station and bought a ticket for the three-hour ride to Brighton. As he sat waiting for the train, he thought about the woman who shook his hand and thanked him. *Would it have mattered to her had she known he spent the war as a prisoner?* He remembered the devastation he saw as he marched across Germany. *Without the support of Canadian troops, that scene might well have been England.* The noisy arrival of a train interrupted his thoughts. He rose and picked up his haversack.

Ten minutes later, a taxi pulled up to the curb.

"Keep the change," said Jean-Pierre as he handed the driver a one-pound note and exited the cab.

He straightened his shoulders and walked briskly towards the Aldershot camp entrance, determined to address his fears. A guard at the gate gave him directions to the Fusiliers' headquarters and administrative office. When he reached the building, Jean-Pierre paused, took a deep breath, and entered. He recognised the sergeant major seated behind the desk at the far end of the room. He removed his cap, took three steps to the front of the desk, placed his haversack on the floor, and snapped to attention.

"Lance Corporal Laekas reporting for duty, Sergeant Major," said Jean-Pierre in a strong voice that masked his feelings.

The Sergeant Major looked up from the paperwork on the desk.

"Managed to find your own way here, did you?"

"Yes Sergeant Major."

The sergeant major nodded, put down his pen, and rose from his seat. He walked around the desk and extended his hand. Jean-Pierre took it, uncertain of why he wanted to shake his hand.

"Welcome home Fusilier," said the sergeant major with a broad smile. "Your regiment is very proud of you."

The End

M.F.M. 267
50M-9-44 (5634)
H.Q. 1772-33-1989

CANADIAN NATIONAL
TELEGRAPHS

MM

FILE H.Q.   405-L-8707

OTTAWA   12 MAY 1945

CASUALTY (REPORT DELIVERY)

TO:- MR MICHEL LAEKAS
1793 BEAUDRY
MONTREAL QUE

PLEASED TO INFORM YOU THAT D61894 LANCE

CORPORAL JEAN PIERRE LAEKAS   PREVIOUSLY REPORTED PRISONER

OF WAR GERMANY NOW OFFICIALLY REPORTED SAFE IN UNITED KINGDOM

TENTH MAY 1945   STOP ADDRESS MAIL LIBERATED PRISONER OF WAR

CANADIAN ARMY OVERSEAS STOP WHEN FURTHER INFORMATION BECOMES

AVAILABLE IT WILL BE FORWARDED AS SOON AS RECEIVED

PREPAID

DIRECTOR OF RECORDS

Telegram from the Canadian Army to Jean-Pierre's father notifying him of Jean-Pierre's liberation. *Private Collection.*

224

DIEPPE

It was on the eighteenth of August, in nineteen-forty-two,
We sailed away from England, and no one knew where to.
We had received no orders, no friends to see us leave,
The Second Canadian Division, with the blue patch on our sleeve.

Early next morning, when everything was still
We saw the tracer bullets, come at us from the hill,
But we kept right on sailing, and no man will forget
The morning that we landed, on the beach there at Dieppe.

The enemy were waiting, and had taken up their posts,
We met a hail of bullets, as we landed on the coast,
But every man there landed, or at least he tried,
Though many there were wounded, and many more men died.

It was early in the morning when we started in to fight,
The mortar bombs came at us, from the left and from the right.
They shelled us from the cliffs and bombed us from the air,
But the Second Canadian Division was not so easily scared.

We fought there for nine hours, from five a.m. to two,
Our losses were terrific, but there was nothing we could do.
The Navy came to help us, but their boats they couldn't land,
So we had to surrender, at Dieppe there on the sand.

What is left of us are prisoners, beneath a foreign flag,
Here in the heart of Germany, at camp VIIIB, stalag.
Many of our comrades fell, but we will never forget,
That they gave their lives there fighting, in the Battle of Dieppe.

When the war is over, and once again we're free,
To our homes we will be sailing, to the land of liberty.
Though many of us have a battle scar, no man will forget,
The morning that we landed, on the French coast at Dieppe.

Written in Stalag VIIIB by Sapper Barnes, C.W., 2nd Field Coy, R.C.E. (B-25330)

Epilogue

Arthur Fraser

Following his discharge from the hospital in England, Arthur boarded a ship with a large contingent of Canadian soldiers destined for Halifax, Nova Scotia. During the trip home, Arthur played the dice game, Crown & Anchor. He paid a soldier to bring him his food and drinks, only breaking for the bathroom and catnaps. After five days of gambling, his winnings totalled over 700 pounds sterling (more than $2,500 in Canadian dollars). To circumvent the regulation limiting Canadian soldiers to 100 pounds sterling upon entry into Canada, Arthur hired six soldiers to each take ashore 100 pounds. After the ship had docked, Arthur's family and friends waved and called to him from behind the wire mesh fence. Arthur waved back and then turned his attention to the soldiers exiting the customs and immigration, searching for the six men who had his money.

Arthur married and settled in the Montréal area. He supported the Dieppe Veterans Association until he passed away in April 2012.

Maurice Jolicoeur

In 1945, Maurice left the hospital and planned to visit the Lyon family in Glasgow. A telephone call from his brother changed those plans. His brother flew transport aircraft for the Royal Air Force and asked if Maurice would like to fly with him to Egypt. His brother provided him an aircrew outfit and they flew to Cairo. Though warned against drinking cold Egyptian beer in the heat of the day, the radio operator had and was hospitalised. The rest of the crew went touring while he recovered. Maurice rode a camel to the pyramids of Giza, near the burial site of the pharaohs Khufu, Khafre, and Menkaure. He also led the group on a climb up one of the pyramids. When he reached the top, he marked his conquest by urinating from the peak. He and his brother carved their names in the ancient limestone before they descended. Within a few days, the wireless operator recovered and they flew back to England. When Maurice returned to his regiment, he received a reprimand for being absent without leave and a demotion in rank.

Maurice returned to Canada, married his St. Lambert girlfriend Pierrette Pelletier, and together they raised a large and loving family. Maurice continues to share his war experiences with French Canadian youths. I have maintained the friendship with Maurice and Pierrette that developed during my interviews for this story. When I visit, Maurice prepares our meal while Pierrette and I listen attentively to tales of his incredible wartime adventures.

Jean-Pierre Laekas

On 13 September 1945, Jean-Pierre married Mary Doreen Baker at the Registrar's Office in Brighton. Jean-Pierre returned to Montréal to obtain his discharge from the Fusiliers Mont-Royal on 14 November 1945. He went back to England and lived in a beautiful little house by the sea with his wife Mary and his son Michael John. Mary gave birth to Annabelle in 1946 and Adrian in 1948. Three months later, Jean-Pierre returned to Canada with Mary and their young family. They were blessed with three more children, Peter in 1949, and twins Stephanie and Beverly in 1952. Despite some difficult financial years when he struggled to provide for his family, he somehow found the means to continue, just as he had as a prisoner of war. Jean-Pierre became a successful businessman, recognised for his marketing skills. He was an avid sportsman and a devoted husband and father. He enjoyed an active social life and sang in the church choir. He gave selflessly to all those in need and was a member of the Dieppe Veterans Association. In later years, his health began to fail when he developed Parkinson's disease and the memories of his wartime experiences returned to haunt him.

Jean-Pierre Laekas passed away on 4 March 2002. His beloved Mary joined him on 9 September 2011. They share a common gravestone at the Last Post National Field of Honour in Beaconsfield, Quebec.

Acknowledgements

I owe a deep gratitude to the following people and institutions that provided information and material for this story.

Arthur Fraser, Maurice Jolicoeur, and my father, Jean-Pierre Laekas, three veterans of the raid on Dieppe, France

Mr. Caillet, his son Alain, and Mme Inge Becq of the Mémorial du 19 août 1942 museum in Dieppe, France

Anna Wickiewicz of the Central Prisoner of War Museum in Labinowice, Poland (site of Stalag VIIIB)

Piotr Stanek of the Central Prisoner of War Museum in Opole, Poland

Piotr Tarnawski of the Stargard Museum in Stargard, Poland

Kevin Greenhalgh curator of the Stalag XIB Museum in Bad Fallingbostel, Germany

The librarians and archivists at Library and Archives Canada, Ottawa, Canada; the Canadian War Museum, Ottawa, Canada; Selfoss Library, Selfoss, Iceland; Gourock Library, Gourock, Scotland; Mitchell Library, Glasgow, Scotland; Lancing College Library, Lancing, England; Aldershot Military Museum, Aldershot, England; Verneuil Library, Verneuil-sur-Seine, France.

Last but not least, I want to thank my wonderful wife Johanne, whose unwavering encouragement, support, drive, and expertise are the reasons this book exists.

Michael John Laekas

Bibliography

Before writing this story, I read a number of publications on the Dieppe raid to gain a better appreciation of the military and political aspects before, during, and after Operation Jubilee.

Calin, Harold. Dieppe. New York: Tower Publications, Inc., 1978.

Dancocks, Daniel G. In Enemy Hands. Edmonton: Hurtig Publishers Ltd., 1983.

DeFelice, Jim. Ranger at Dieppe. New York: Penguin Group, 2008.

Ford, Ken. Dieppe 1942 Prelude to D-Day. Oxford: Osprey Publishing Ltd., 2003.

Juteau, Paul. Unpublished Manuscript No 30. 1995.

Maguire, Eric. Dieppe August 19. London: Transworld Publishers Ltd., 1963.

Mellor, John. Forgotten Heroes. Agincourt: Methuen Publications, 1975.

Mordal, Jacques. Dieppe – The Dawn of Decision. London: New English Library Limited, 1981.

Neillands, Robin. The Dieppe Raid. London: Aurum Press Limited, 2006.

Robertson, Terrance. Dieppe: The Shame and The Glory. London: Hutchinson & Co. Ltd., 1965.

Vennat, Pierre. Les Fusiliers Mont-Royal. Online Internet Site.

Villa, Brian Loring. Unauthorized Action. Don Mills: Oxford University Press, 1990.

Whitaker, Brigadier General Denis and Shelagh Whitaker. Dieppe – Tragedy to Triumph. Whitby: McGraw-Hill Ryerson Limited, 1992.

_____. Cent ans d'histoire d'un Régiment canadien-français Les Fusiliers Mont-Royal 1869-1969. Montréal: Éditions du jour Inc., 1971.

About The Author

Michael John Laekas is the author of four other published books that pay tribute to his parents, Mary and John Laekas. In 2009, he embarked on a project to provide a legacy for future generations. The result is a set of books that will appeal to fans of stories about love, war, and family. First came the trilogy *Mary and John, The Early Years* that describes the rough and tumble world of his parents, from their childhood to young adults. Then he created *Reliving Their Journey,* a remarkable photo album with narrative that followed his emotional 47-day visit to places in Canada, Great Britain, and Europe that marked significant events in his parents' young lives.

Front cover
Jean-Pierre Laekas, POW # 26652, at Stalag IID in Stargard, Poland, 1944.

Back cover
Les Fusiliers Mont-Royal badge

The crown represents service to the Sovereign. The grenade alludes to the original role of fusiliers, who were soldiers specially equipped to escort artillery trains. "FMR" is the abbreviation of the regimental title and "NUNQUAM RETRORSUM" is the motto of the regiment, which means "Never Retreat".

www.ingramcontent.com/pod-product-compliance
Lightning Source LLC
Chambersburg PA
CBHW060235050426
42448CB00009B/1446